A PRIEST FROM THE
PRAIRIES OF MINNESOTA

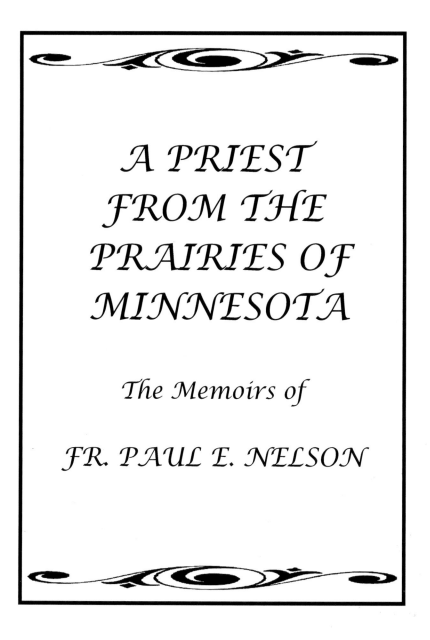

A PRIEST FROM THE PRAIRIES OF MINNESOTA

The Memoirs of

FR. PAUL E. NELSON

Published by GRANDOC PUBLISHING
grandoc@mac.com

ISBN 978-0-9761739-3-9

Library of Congress Control Number: 2011940751

ACKNOWLEDGMENTS

I extend a sincere "Thank you" to Dr. John Graner, my friend, who challenged me, encouraged me, and supported my efforts, as I wrote these memoirs. He also has proven himself to be an excellent editor and organizer of my ideas. I am also grateful to my friends, Sharon Manahan and Lisa and Greg Storey, who read the manuscript, made suggestions, and offered encouragement throughout these last months of researching, remembering and writing. The many people with whom I have worked over fifty years as a priest have contributed to my story and have been a significant part of my life. Thank you to all!

Paul E. Nelson

CONTENTS

SECTION II: PRIEST AND EDUCATOR

SECTION V: THE SPIRITUAL LIFE AND FURTHER REFLECTIONS ON THE SACRAMENTS

SECTION VI: THE CHURCH IN THE MODERN WORLD

SECTION VIII: FINAL REFLECTIONS

ILLUSTRATIONS

FORWARD

I am honored beyond words to write this forward for my friend, Fr. Paul Nelson. Fr. Paul is a well-known (might I say famous?- he would hate me saying that!) and beloved individual in southeastern Minnesota. Very few of us are privileged to have done as much as Paul has for his people. And Paul does indeed consider the people of this region *his* people. He loves all of us very much. This I know from our numerous, intense and highly enjoyable discussions.

Because he is so well-known and loved, our luncheon meetings are often punctuated by one or more individuals coming up to say hello to him. Always loving, always brimming with gratitude- that is what I see in these people's faces. This is something I have never experienced before. I have worked with some famous people, but I have never seen anything like this kind of recognition. Amazing. If you attended his Fiftieth Anniversary Celebration at St. Pius X Parish you experienced firsthand this love and affection. I could not believe the length of those lines!

Let me say also that I have lived in a variety of places over the years, and I can truly say that I have never met such a wise, and at the same time happy, person as Paul. If the priesthood was made for anyone, it was made for him. He loves his job- absolutely *loves* it. A perfect fit. And, of course, this has been a blessing not only for him, but for everyone whose life he touches.

Paul was born and raised on a farm right here amongst us. As you will see when you read this book, since Paul took his first breath he has loved everyone and everything around him: his family, nature, his work, all of the people he has lived with and worked with- all of the people he has worked *for*. Paul is as much a part of this region as are the fields, the sky, the rain. A true man of the people, one *with* the people.

Paul never lets a personal tragedy or hardship get him down too much. In such moments he always turns outward, rather than inward. That is his secret. He turns to the people around him to help *them* at these moments, rather than trying to help himself. And by helping others, he finds his own salvation. I see this as one of the key lessons I learned from reading and preparing this book.

Another lesson I learned from Paul (and this is really a variation on a theme perhaps first set in writing by Aristotle), is that happiness comes through action, by living the virtuous life. You are happy when you are acting in the public space in a virtuous way. That is the happiness that he experiences right now. A win-win situation: he is happy working with people, and he helps and cheers many in the process.

Some editorial notes: What you are about to read is more a series of reflections and observations than it is what I would call a "standard" autobiography. Oh sure, he discusses the basic history of his life, and he has included a goodly number of photographs. But there is *much more* here. Paul is a man with very strong viewpoints, with very strong loves, very profound observations. I sincerely hope that these show through even stronger than do the bare facts and history of his life. And I think they do.

I would say, pay particular attention to how he returns to a few basic themes. He touches down on them, circles around for a while, and then touches down and expands on them again. Those themes are, among others, the Sacraments, the stages of life, the importance of the selfless and active life. (The Sacraments, especially, are such an important theme that, although two of the sections bear that title because they concentrate on various of the Sacraments in more detail, in a real sense this entire book centers around them.) Paul often goes back to a part of his life that he has mentioned earlier, but in a different light, always emphasizing these themes. Watch for that. It is uplifting, to say the least!

One more thing: I have in certain places rear-ranged things a bit from the manuscripts Paul gave me, in order to provide a more continuous story for you, the reader. But I have done this sparingly, and only when I considered it absolutely necessary. What you will read, what I *want* you to read, in this book are Fr. Paul's own thoughts, with but a bare minimum of editing.

John Graner, MD

P.S. Paul is well known for his great homilies, and we had planned to include a number of them at the end of this book. But due to size considerations, we have decided to present them in a separate publica-tion which we hope to have ready shortly after the present volume is released. I would heartily recom-mend that book to you as well.

SECTION I

MY YOUNGER YEARS

CHAPTER 1

Beginnings

In 1935 Social Security was passed into law, Alcoholics Anonymous was established, the first (five pound!) hearing aid was invented, and Paul Edward Nelson was born to Claude and Lenora (O'Connell) Nelson. I was the first of four sons, the others being Bernard, James, and Richard.

I was born at Saint Marys Hospital in Rochester, Minnesota, and began my life's journey on my parents' farm, located four miles south of Mayo High School on County Road 1. I lived there until the age of seven. My childhood life was happy, secure, and exciting.

My father's parents were Peter and Elizabeth (Moulton) Nelson. My grandfather Nelson was Danish, my grandmother Nelson, British. They had seven children: Ida, Lillian ("Curly"), Violet ("Blondie"), Margaret ("Mutt"), Claude (my father), Irvin ("Bud"), and Theodore ("Ted").

My father was wonderful, and all of my aunts and uncles and their spouses were great and enjoyable people. As it turned out, my father, Irvin, Ted, and Margaret were Catholics, while Ida, Lillian and Violet were Lutheran. As a priest I was privileged to officiate at both of my parents' funerals, and to be a part of all of my aunts' and uncles' funerals as well, in either the Catholic or Lutheran setting.

On my mother's side of the family, my grandparents were John and Mary (Dilworth) O'Connell. Both of them were Irish, so I am apparently one-fourth Danish, one-fourth British, and one-half Irish. Grandpa O'Connell died before I was born, but Grandma O'Connell lived with our family for many of my young years. She became a powerful influence on me. Her kindness, faith, bright mind and young spirit taught me much about aging happily, about social outreach, about respect for all of God's creation and people, and about being an active part of the community.

Grandpa and Grandma O'Connell had four daughters: Florence, Lenora (my mother), Ruth, and Gertrude ("Gert"). My mother and my aunts were always very good to me. I was also privileged to officiate at all of their funerals, as well as that of Ruth's husband, my Uncle Bud (also mentioned above- my father's brother), and Gert's husband, my Uncle Robert.

On June 5, 1934, my mother and her sister Ruth married my father and his brother Irvin (Bud) in a double ceremony held at St. Bridget's Church, near Simpson, Minnesota. The two couples began their families on two separate farms near Simpson, and at one point in the mid-forties our two families lived together in a large farm house for more than a year, as they reorganized their finances. Each family had four children, but by the time the families were living together, the oldest son of Bud and Ruth had passed away. John Nelson died at age four.

Our double cousins have all remained close, both emotionally and socially. I have witnessed the weddings of most of my nieces and cousins, baptized most of their children and their children's children. Soon I will participate in my first cousin Don Quandt's funeral in his Lutheran Church near Grand Meadow, Minnesota. I must say that my journey through life with my extended family has been both a peaceful and a growing experience.

Reflections On Growing Up On a Farm

Looking back after 75 years, I strongly believe that a happy and secure childhood was the factor most responsible for my happiness and success throughout life. Of course, my family had its share of pressures, disagreements and sad days, but for the most part we were at peace- working, talking, and truly listening to each other. While working together we laughed together. Some of our favorite pastimes were listening to the radio, and making wish lists of the things we saw in the shiny pages of the Sears Robuck catalogue.

Life before television was different. We had to talk and listen to each other, sharing the simple pleasures of the home and remaining aware of the reality and possibilities inherent in the present moment. Our imaginations were challenged by the movements of the things of nature rather than the distractions of the television marketplace.

We lived with outhouses rather than bathrooms, using candles and lanterns for light. We carried fresh water into the house and the used water out of the house. We carried wood in for the stove, and carried the ashes out every day.

We felt close to nature. The weather and the changes in life around us were of prime importance to our well-being. We were conscious of living close to the earth, of being totally dependent upon it. And the earth was full of truly exciting phenomena. Living with the plants, animals, rodents, birds and bats was a profoundly beautiful experience.

The earth was also a wonderful teacher for me. It never speaks a word, but constantly communicates through its movements and changes, its generating of new life. For me growing up, it was the home of God. It was the place of power, from which new life sprang every year. It was the stage of mystery, holding a truth more profound than any human mind could comprehend.

The trees spoke to me in a special way. I loved to feel their buds as the spring gave them new life. The sap rose to give new foliage and strength to the limbs, ultimately bearing new fruit to enrich the rest of life. The trees seemed to be proud of the fact that although not praised, or perhaps even noticed much, they were always there to provide the rest of creation with shade, fruit, nuts, berries, and of course oxygen.

Trees know they provide free housing for all of the birds, squirrels, chipmunks, bees, bugs, and little creatures that in some way contribute to the balance of the earth, in order that life may continue productively and naturally. I learned that the ecosystem of the earth is a balanced and delicate, powerful and vulnerable one, requiring the knowledge, the prudence, the wisdom of humanity to protect it, to work with it, to respect it, and so to contribute to the future of the earth and its creatures.

Perennial flowers have always been an interest of mine. Watching the tulips spring up, even through the snow, and waiting for them to bloom in their bright-colored pride, was an image of hope and of new life.

What a joy it was to find the nests of ducks in hidden places, and to watch the nests of chickens and ducks, waiting for the magical day when peeping could be heard from under the mother. As a child, I found baby chicks and ducklings mesmerizing.

Baby rabbits begin to hop around in the spring. And little birds sit on the lawn, bewildered by this new experience, and by the task of learning to fly- and landing without crashing! Small young squirrels venture out from the safely of their nests in the trees on a quest of discovery of the new and different. Equally intriguing was the anticipation of the birth of the calves, piglets, kittens, and sometimes colts and puppies, as spring appeared and the weather warmed.

Yes, growing up on the farm was a blessing that I never could have orchestrated, that I did not, during my youth, fully appreciate. But I have since come to know that living close to nature, and being daily involved with it, is the greatest gift that I could have hoped for.

We are one with creation as we are one with the Creator. We do not understand or comprehend this. We simply appreciate that mystery, participating in it, and through that participation, grow in depth day by day- grow in the sharing, day by day.

I remember that one of the most stimulating educational moments in my young life was when Dad told me about fertilizer. I must have asked him why we spread smelly cow manure over the fields. Would it not poison the crops for the next year? He assured me that if we did not return its nutrients to the earth, then indeed there would be no crops! This revelation led me to study this process. I remember referring to the encyclopedia at Lourdes Junior/Senior High School (no Internet in those days!) to learn more about this. I learned how the earth's waste, when properly managed and recycled, was what provided us with new life and continued existence.

This was a great moment for me. I became even more bound to the earth, and less embarrassed about being called a "dumb farmer". I was proud to know something of the mysteries of our existence demonstrated through the chemical cycles that gave me a "big picture" of life on earth.

The weather, then and now, has remained a challenge to predict. The difference was that back then, in the forties and fifties, we listened to the radio for a description of the weather conditions, and for the predictions that may or may not become reality.

CHAPTER 2

Childhood Anecdotes

The first incident I remember from my early life involved our first bicycle. Bernard and I had both wanted one, so our father bought us a used girl's bicycle painted drab blue. I remember that when we rode it we took a lot of abuse from our farm neighbors and friends. Also, before I became an experienced rider, I ran over a chicken in our yard, killing it- not a happy memory!

When I was six years old, in 1941, My father's banker, Lester Fuegel, asked him if I could take care of his son's rabbits. His son had been drafted into the army, World War II having just begun. My father told Lester that I would be glad to care for his son's rabbits, and so I became the proud, albeit temporary, owner of three purebreds- two white doe females and one white buck.

I fell in love with those rabbits, and began to acquire other breeds. Rabbits are gentle, quiet animals full of energy. They love to hop! They are also vulnerable, trusting and seemingly naïve. I discovered they also reproduce rapidly! The result of this latter discovery was that my rabbits began very quickly to send me little rabbits at a profound pace.

Two or three years went by, Dad patiently helping me with them. Then one fateful spring day, I went to my father crying. The cats on the farm were killing and eating my baby rabbits! My father defended the cats, because they kept the mouse and rat population at bay. He gently but firmly told me that the rabbits had to go. (At this point I owned more than 375 of them!) He helped my mother and me place a cage in the trunk of our 1941 Chevy. In that cage we hauled fifteen rabbits at a time to the Mayo Clinic research farm at Mayowood. I recall crying all the way there on each trip we took, as we ushered my rabbits into the Mayowood Laboratories. I knew full well that they were destined for experimentation in the laboratory, and eventually for death.

My Youthful Education

My formal education began in the spring of 1940, at the age of five. I attended kindergarten in a one-room school house, District #72, located about a mile south of our farm. I liked school, and did well. The building is long gone. There is now no trace that it ever existed.

When I was six years old, my family sold our farm and moved to a larger one. This was located one-half mile south and one-half mile west of Simpson. This move necessitated changing schools, and I began to attend Simpson School District #14. This was a big step up for me, because the school now had two rooms, the "little room" for children in kindergarten through fourth grade, and the "big room" for the so-phisticates- grades five through eight. There were a total of only three students in my grade for my first six years.

At the end of sixth grade, the district announced that it would no longer be able to afford two rooms and two teachers. Seventh and eighth grade students would now have to attend school in Rochester. My pastor, Fr. Pat Farrell, encouraged my parents to send me to Lourdes Junior/Senior High School in that town. My parents had to pay $9.00 a month for me to ride the bus to school. They also had to pay $9.00 a month for Lourdes tuition. This was a large outlay for poor farmers. Their decision to send me to Lourdes was a very important one for me and my subsequent career. I received a superb education at Lourdes under the auspices of the good Sisters of St. Francis of

Rochester. The sisters were well versed in the art and science of pedagogy, fair but strict disciplinarians, and careful directors of young people. They guided us well in our emotional, spiritual, psychological, and sexual development. The foundations of my education first in small rural public schools, and subsequently at Lourdes Junior and Senior High School, set me on a path of success for the rest of my life.

CHAPTER 3

Work On the Farm

One day, when I was nine or ten, my dad said to me and my brother Bernard, who was three years younger than I, "It is time for you boys to learn how to work. One of you can help me with the cattle, hogs and horses, and the other one can help your mother in the kitchen and garden, and with the chickens." We had about three hundred smelly chickens.

Since I was the older, I got to choose first. I remember vividly that I said, "I want to help you in the barn, Dad," and that pleased Bernard, who hated the barn and everything that went with it. He was delighted to help in the house and garden, but somewhat less enthusiastic about dealing with the chickens. So both of us began our working careers satisfied and happy.

Our family had a herd of twenty-eight Holstein cattle and ten sows that pigged on schedule. I aided in the birth of many a calf, extending my arm into the birth canal to turn the unborn calf so that it could exit the womb feet and nose first. I also picked up new-born pigs to massage them in order to assist them in the breathing process.

We had a team of horses, Maggie and Jigs. They were big, gentle and powerful. I loved to curie them. This process entails removing the loose hairs from their bodies with a steel brush, so they would remain clean and not itch. These simple experiences somehow gave me a profound respect for nature, life and basic being. In hindsight I must say that in some respect these farming activities provided me more education than any college or university course could provide.

The daily routine on the farm began with Dad awakening me at 4:45 AM. We would dress for the barn, and go there to greet, feed and tend to the cattle. We would cleanse the cows' utters and then milk them.

Processing the milk was a discipline in itself. We had to protect its purity by making sure it got to the milk house quickly. (The milk house was a small room just off the barn.) It was placed into the cooling tank immediately. Part of my responsibility each morning and night was thoroughly washing the milking machine, the tit cups, pails, and all of the equipment used in acquiring milk from the cows. I would also transport the milk to the cooler, making certain that the cooler lid was clean and functioning properly.

We also cleaned the barn daily. We would shovel the cow manure from the gutters behind the cows into a manure spreader, and would hose down the areas where urine and feces had been. After this we would sweep lime over the entire area. The purpose of the lime was to neutralize any bacteria that may be hiding in the milk producing area.

Dad was an excellent farmer, and took his responsibility very seriously. Inspectors never questioned the quality of his milk. Dad was never mean to me, but he insisted that I do my work in the barn with the cattle correctly, responsibly, and thoroughly. Shortcuts were never tolerated. This was a profound foundation for my life, and I am humbly grateful to my parents for their training, discipline, and direction.

At age ten, my father taught me to drive a team of horses to spread manure. We did the spreading daily, so that it could nurture the land and increase our crop yield the following year.

Also at the age of ten, my father taught me to drive a tractor and a truck. In the spring I would cultivate corn. I drove up and down the rows of corn with the tractor, cultivator attached, to remove weeds. I learned to pay very close attention so as not to wander off the row I was driving and destroy the crop of corn or soybeans I was seeking to protect. My father taught me also how to change oil in the tractors and check the other fluids before starting the engine- all part of keeping the machines in good order.

At the age of twelve I began to haul grain from our combine, which my father was operating in the field, to the elevator in Stewartville ten miles away. There the grain was weighed and unloaded. I was given a receipt, and I would then drive back to the farm and pick up another load of grain. My father taught me never to drive over twenty miles per hour, a rule that I obeyed scrupulously, since I am alive to tell about it!

Another thing I learned to do at the age of twelve was to climb the outside of the silo. It was the fall of the year, and Dad asked me to assist him in directing the flow of the snout of the silage pipe blower into the roof of the silo. To place the blower pipe correctly into the silo required a person on the ground and a person in the cage on the top of the silo. The chopped corn silage we blew into the silo was used to feed the cattle during the winter.

Now, the silo on our farm was a good forty-five feet high. On its outside was a narrow ladder leading all the way to the top. My father put me on the ladder in front of him. We climbed together with his arms around me, grabbing the ladder on each side. His advice to me was, "Never look straight up. If there are clouds moving, they may disorient you; never look straight down, because you will fear the distance between yourself and the ground. Rather, always look at the horizon. That view will give you equilibrium and empower you to keep climbing without fear." I have never forgotten that advice, and am not afraid of heights to this day.

A Tragic Incident

I would like to pause for a moment to relate a tragic incident that also occurred when I was twelve years old. Each year Father Patrick Farrell, the aforementioned pastor of St. Bridget's Catholic Church, took the altar servers on a day picnic. In the summer of 1947 he decided to treat the twelve of us to something special on this picnic, which was held at Sandy Point Resort, located about twelve miles north of Rochester on the Zumbro River. He had rented a motor boat and took us on a boat ride.

Before that day, I don't think that any of us had ridden in a boat. The boat could comfortably hold seven, so Father Farrell took six of us at a time on a fifteen-minute ride. We were instructed to sit for the entire ride, and not to stand until he had beached the boat at the end of the ride. In those days life jackets were rarely used, and we had none on our boat.

I was in the second group of boys, and we had been playing in the water near the shore of the resort for about an hour before the boat returned for our ride. Lake Zumbro is an old rocky quarry, and although the first forty feet of water out from the shore was no more than three feet in depth, at about forty-five feet out it dropped off to forty feet in depth.

As we returned at the end of our ride, but were still well off from shore, my third cousin Clarence O'Connell stood up and jumped out of the boat! Poor Clarence disappeared below the water, and by the time Fr. Farrell could beach the boat and dive for Clarence he was lost. Clarence's brother Richard had witnessed this terrible accident and was deeply traumatized. Needless to say, we all were. There was no phone near the beach, and so Fr. Farrell had to drive to the nearest farm to call the fire department for help.

The Rochester fire department arrived about a half-hour later. They dragged the lake bottom and soon found Clarence's drowned body. This was the most traumatic, painful and frightening day of my young life. The next few days before the funeral were terribly sad, frightening and confusing. Although this accident occurred almost sixty-four years ago, I still remember it graphically, as though it had been yesterday.

CHAPTER 4

More Stories of My Youth

4-H was a strong program at this time, especially for the children of farm families. My parents got us involved with it as soon as we became eligible, and I enjoyed several projects over the years. I had great success with garden exhibits as well as the showing of Angus beef calves. I also participated in the Tractor Mechanics program for a couple of years, and at one point won a trip to Chicago to attend the national meeting of 4-H leaders. I remember that we stayed at the Conrad Hilton Hotel on Lake Street, thinking that I must be a big boy indeed, having come all the way from Simpson, Minnesota to stay in this place.

As the years passed I assumed more responsibilities on the farm. I learned to operate all of the equipment for planting, nurturing the crops, and harvesting. Bailing hay for the winter food for the cattle and horses was very hot, dusty and hard work. We also bailed straw after the grain was harvested. This was used to provide our animals clean bedding throughout the winter.

I learned how to harness the team of horses, how to calm them around running machinery, and how to perform the tasks their massive strength could accomplish. I was a good horseman, but did experience two runaways. This is when the horses take off at a gallop, frightened and out of control. I was not injured during these episodes - only my pride was hurt.

Both of these runaways occurred while I was on a wagon loaded with grain bundles that I was preparing to place in the threshing machine hopper. I was lucky that the wagon did not tip over during either of these episodes. I was eventually able to calm the horses as they tired from their long run, and as we distanced ourselves from the noisy threshing machines. I was always humble when driving a team of horses. They are powerful, intelligent creatures that react instinctively and immediately when they perceive danger; and two tons of horses can always exert their will over a 150 pound man.

I must say that I was more interested in farming than I was in academics during my high school years at Lourdes. In the 1940's and 1950's, almost all farm work was done manually. We threw silage from the silo every day to feed the cattle and other livestock. We then distributed the silage to the animals in the barn using a wheelbarrow. This combined with the various milking chores mentioned previously resulted in a great deal of manual labor. Consequently, I did not study as hard or as thoroughly as I may have done otherwise. Nonetheless, I did well in school, receiving the "All Around Student" award at graduation. I was to learn better study habits in college.

I can't say enough about the benefits of growing up on a dairy farm. I learned how to work hard, intelligently and responsibly. I learned how to respect nature, the cycles of life, the unity of all creation. I learned that all creation is one, and I learned that the earth is a profound and wonderful mother, able to provide new life each year. I also learned that we must respect Mother Earth, care for her, cleanse her.

Life on the farm was a lot of work, but it was not all work. We had many wonderful times. One evening, when I was about fifteen years old, Shorty Caflisch, a friend and neighbor, picked Richard O'Connell and myself up in his car. We went driving around the countryside. After a bit of time discussing what we three poor, Catholic, country boys would do that night, we naturally devised the scheme of stealing watermelons!

We eventually discovered a watermelon field and started sneaking through it. We decided upon a large, beautiful melon. I was assigned the task of carrying it back to the car. I was hefting it along when the farmer whose field we were in discovered us. He quickly fired a shotgun blast over our heads to scare us off. As I fled to the car, I dropped the melon. It fell into pieces. Shorty was very upset that I could not even secure our stolen property long enough to get to his car. This was not one of our happiest nights together.

The Beginnings of My Spiritual Journey

My spiritual journey began with my baptism at St. Bridget's Catholic Church, located near the small village of Simpson. My God Parents were my mother's sister Gert and my father's brother Ted. I remained fond of them throughout their lives.

My family always attended Mass on Sundays and Holy Days. When there was too much snow to drive on the country roads that passed our house, I remember going to church in a sleigh pulled by our horses, Maggy and Jigs. We wrapped ourselves in heavy blankets to keep warm.

I received my Sacraments at St. Bridget's. I received First Communion at the age of seven, and Confirmation around the age of ten.

When I was sixteen years old, my maternal grandmother began keeping house for Fr. Farrell. Since our family lived only a mile from the church and rectory, we boys would ride our bicycles there to see Grandma several times a week. She always had chocolate chip cookies waiting for us in great and unrestricted quantities, which may help to explain why we chose to visit her so often.

During one of these visits, when I was a junior in high school, Fr. Farrell called me into his office for a chat. Eventually he got around to the point. He said, "Paul, have you ever thought of becoming a priest?" I happened to be sweet on a girl in my class at Lourdes at the time, and the issue of celibacy immediately came to mind. I politely informed Fr. Farrell that I did not think I wanted to be a priest. He countered by saying something like, "Well Paul, you have the qualities that are needed to be an effective priest. I want you to pray about it."

After that encounter I never had a comfortable moment as an adolescent boy. I somehow knew that I could serve people as a priest. Another year went by, and in the spring of my senior year in high school, again while visiting my grandmother, Fr. Farrell called me into his office and told me he thought I should enter the seminary.

Mainly because I respected Fr. Farrell and did not wish to disappoint him, I made the decision to try the seminary for a year. I applied to, and was accepted at, the Immaculate Heart of Mary Seminary, a subdivision of St. Mary's College in Winona, Minnesota. My parents took me to the seminary in early September of 1953.

I cried myself to sleep every night for the first three months. Homesickness hit me very hard, and I was too embarrassed to speak of it to my friends or my superiors. I finally broke that dependent emotional attachment to my parents, siblings, and the way of life I had known. Once I got through that, I was able to spend four very happy years at Immaculate Heart of Mary Seminary. I studied philosophy and the liberal arts, and graduated from St. Mary's College in the spring of 1957 with a BA in Philosophy and minors in Classical Languages (Latin and Greek) and Education. Bishop Fitzgerald, the then Bishop of Winona, met with me and my classmates and assigned us to graduate schools (seminaries) in the spring of 1957. I was assigned to Saint Paul Seminary in Saint Paul, Minnesota. I was to study Theology for the next four years. While at Saint Paul, I studied Dogmatic Theology, Moral Theology, Pastoral Theology, Church History, Canon Law (Church Law), Liturgy, Catechetics, Sacramental Theology, and other subjects pertaining to the life of the Catholic Church.

I hated almost every day at that seminary. Discipline was horribly strict, academics merely adequate but not excellent. In such an atmosphere trust between students, as well as between staff and students, was minimal. I thank God frequently that I could survive that period of my young life. I have had fifty years of happiness as a priest, so I try not to judge the place too harshly-I *try*, anyway.

My classmates and I left Saint Paul Seminary on May 26, 1961. We stayed overnight in a Dominican monastery located in the Hills of Winona, and the following day were ordained priests by Bishop Edward A. Fitzgerald in the Cathedral of the Sacred Heart, in Winona.

I returned home to the farm after that, and realized that I was frightened to death. I thought, "I can't do this!" I asked myself, "Who will listen to me?", "Who do I think I am?", "I am a 'head case' to think that I belong in this job!"

SECTION II

PRIEST AND EDUCATOR

CHAPTER 5

In the Gospel Trenches

Our diocese, the Diocese of Winona, is comprised of a belt of counties across southern Minnesota, from Wisconsin to South Dakota, a total of twenty-three counties in all. Thankfully, I was sent to St. Augustine Parish in Austin, Minnesota as my first assignment. I was to teach Religion full-time at Pacelli High School. Luckily, I landed in a house with four other priests, a kindly house keeper, an understanding pastor (Monsignor Robert Jennings), and a very capable principal at Pacelli (Fr. John Tighe).

Thus I began a professional journey that was to last fifty years. It could not have been more fulfilling, more challenging, more exciting, or more satisfying for me. I traveled the paths of priesthood, teacher, principal of three of our diocesan high schools, Superintendent of Diocesan Schools, Professor of Theology at St. Mary's College in Winona, Chaplain at the College of St. Teresa in Winona, and Newman Center Chaplain at Winona State University.

I did all this by taking it one day at a time, learning to stay in the present moment, learning to appreciate the scene, the circumstances, the personalities, and the current issues. This was a challenge, testing all that I had. Mostly, I succeeded. Infrequently, I failed. Always I had advisors, mentors, friends and colleagues near to help me succeed or to recover from my failures, bad judgments, and mistakes.

I spent 1961 to the summer of 1964 at St. Augustine, and teaching at Pacelli High School. I began to get some administrative experience while there, because I was asked to serve as Athletic Director. Also, during the summers of these years, Bishop Fitzgerald assigned me to begin graduate school at St. Mary's University in Winona, studying Educational Administration.

In the summer of 1964, I was re-assigned from Austin to Winona. My assignments were to work as a teacher of religion at Cotter High School, as Assistant Pastor for St. John's Parish in Winona, and as Assistant Director of Religious Education for the diocese. I was to give each of these responsibilities a third of my attention. It was a happy, but difficult, year.

I received my Masters degree in Educational Administration at the end of the summer of 1965, and was assigned as Principal of Cotter High School. At that time the school had six hundred students and approximately fifty full and part-time staff people. My ten years there were among the happiest of my life. I was successful, and learned a great deal about education, administration, discipline, human relations, spirituality, and team work.

A Couple of Athletic Stories

There are some memorable stories from those years, leading Cotter as principal. Almost every year we held a donkey basketball game to raise money for our athletic department. The seniors would play against the faculty, all riding donkeys. The donkeys were trained to throw people off their backs and make them appear foolish. This is why the activity was such a good money maker! Parents, students and friends packed the gymnasium to enjoy the spectacle. My assignment was always to clean up the excrement left by the donkeys. Of course, the crowd always enjoyed this. Catcalls, comments and other verbal observations were generated at a lively pace, and everyone laughed. I enjoyed the banter, partly because I knew that we were making the big money needed to run our

Athletic department for another year. And having been a farm boy, it was no big deal for me to deal with animal waste.

Another athletic story comes to mind. I had a friend in Winona by the name of Stan Shargy, the father of several children who attended Cotter. Stan had played major league baseball with, among others, Babe Ruth. Unfortunately, he broke his leg during his rookie year in the majors, and that injury ended his major league career.

Stan was a close friend of the top umpire in the American League. The man's name was Nestor Shylock, and he and Stan had been roommates while they played in the majors. Nestor was scheduled to work the Twins game against the Oakland Athletics in Minneapolis in a few days, and Stan invited me to attend the game with him. He also invited me to attend breakfast prior to the game with the Oakland team, of which Joe Dimaggio was one of the major owners. We would also meet with the umpires before the game.

We drove to Minneapolis very early in the morning, and arrived at the old Leamington Hotel at seven AM. We did indeed have breakfast with the team. Stan, Nestor, Joe Dimaggio and I sat together at the same table. I was very interested, as a young man in my thirties, to listen to these famous men, these powerful men of baseball, influential in the conduct of the major leagues. I was happy to see how down to earth they were. After breakfast, Joe asked me to step outside the hotel so that we could be photographed together. After forty years, I still have that photo.

CHAPTER 6

A Sobering Incident in the Schoolyard

Another story is still vivid in my mind after forty years. At the end of each school year, the graduating seniors would finish classes and exams on Wednesday noon, have graduation practice at 2:00 PM, and graduate at 8:00 that evening. The underclass students had another two days of school.

On that Wednesday noon about 1970, after the seniors had finished their classes and were waiting for graduation that evening, a group of five senior boys stood in the middle of the street between the classrooms and the recreational center drinking a fifth of whisky. They were passing the bottle around to each other. There was an audience of about 250 underclassmen standing around them.

One of my staff, a Franciscan Sister, came rushing into my office to inform me of the situation. I hurried out to the street, praying for prudence and a proper authoritative approach to resolve this public issue. I knew that if I did not handle this situation well

I would be finished as a creditable leader for students, staff, and the entire Cotter community.

I walked through the crowd of underclass people and approached the five drinkers. The crowd fell into dead silence. I said to the five boys, loudly enough for all to hear, "Please give me the bottle." The young man holding the bottle immediately handed it to me. I asked, "Where is the cap for the bottle?" One of the other boys produced it from his pocket. I then said to the five of them, again in a voice loud enough for all in the crowd to hear, "I have graduation practice with your class in two hours. If each of you does not show up in my office within the next hour with at least one of your parents, you will not graduate from Cotter High School this year. Now go home and get your parents."

Immediately, in front of everyone, one of the five began crying and sobbing. He said, "I can't get my parents. They are returning from Michigan, and won't be back to Winona until about 4:00." I thought for a moment and then said to him, "Do not come to graduation practice. If your parents contact me personally before graduation, I will consider whether or not you will graduate. Now go home and wait for your parents."

I turned toward the class building, the partially consumed fifth of Jim Beam in hand, and returned to my office. The crowd remained almost perfectly quiet. I knew the story would be told in all of their households that night, and I felt all right about how I had handled things so far.

Within fifteen minutes of the incident, the boys and their parents began filing into my office. When all four sets of students and parents had arrived, I took them into an empty classroom and closed the door. I said to the boys, "Tell your parents what you did a few minutes ago in front of 250 to 300 underclass people." There were tearful and humble confessions, very accurately presented. I said to the boys and to their parents, "You boys broke civil law publicly. You broke the rules of Cotter High School. You did this arrogantly and very publicly, in front of most of the Cotter students. I will allow you to graduate if you and your parents agree to the following plan. Tomorrow morning at 9:00, each of you, along with at least one parent present, will make a public apology to the students and staff in an entire-school assembly. You will further, for the next two weeks, come to Cotter from 8 AM and remain until 4 PM. During that time you will work, doing whatever the custodians ask you to do." All present readily agreed. The parents were most supportive of me and my plan.

When the fifth boy's parents got back to Winona, they came in and readily agreed to the plan.

This was a hardship for the boys because they all had summer jobs lined up, but again, all of the parents agreed that this act, performed so publicly with the underclass people present, had to be handled properly for the sake of the school's reputation. I think this incident was the most difficult disciplinary decision I had to make in all of my years of high school management.

A Family Tragedy

In 1972 I was stationed on a part-time basis at the Immaculate Heart of Mary Seminary, located on the campus of St. Mary's University. I was still the Principal of Cotter. On April 1, 1972, a Holy Saturday, I was on for Easter Vigil ceremonies at the Cathedral in Winona. When the liturgy ended, I went home to the Seminary. The Rector, Bob Brom, met me as I came in from the garage, and told me that he had to talk to me. We entered his office and he closed the door. He asked me to sit down, and then told me that my younger brother Jim had dropped dead in the street in Chatfield after leaving Mass that evening.

I was devastated. I asked Bob to cancel my responsibilities for the next day, Easter morning. Bob was very kind, and handled my entire calendar for the next few days. I drove to my parents' home a few miles away, where my maternal grandmother also lived. She was ninety-four years of age, and had been very close to Jim; they had coffee together every day of the week for many years. We told her that Jim had died.

The next morning I celebrated Mass at home for all of my relatives. This was the most memorable Easter Mass I have ever experienced in my fifty years as a priest. Tonight, April 23, 2011, as I write my thoughts, it is Holy Saturday night. I am not involved in the liturgy tonight, but I am very aware that thirty-nine years ago, on Holy Saturday night, April 1, 1972, Jim came out of Mass at St. Mary's Church in Chatfield, Minnesota accompanied by my brother, Richard. Within minutes of leaving the church, Jim asked Richard, who was driving, to stop at a gas station to get a 7Up from a pop machine to relieve his heartburn. Jim exited the car and fell to the pavement, dead.

On that rainy and cold night, Fr. Frank Enright, the then pastor at St. Mary's, came and stayed with the body of my brother for almost three hours until the authorities could get a coroner to come and announce that Jim was dead of "natural causes." My family has always been most grateful to Fr. Enright for his kind-

ness to my brother Richard that night, and for the respect he had shown for Jim.

I conducted Jim's funeral and burial at St.
Bridget's Church in Simpson. Grandma died three
weeks later. My family and I believe that she died of a
broken heart, over the loss of her grandson and friend.
This is one of the painful stories in my life.

CHAPTER 7

Some Unexpected Guests at Mass

During four of my years as principal at Cotter, I also worked part-time as the Administrator of a small country parish, Saints Peter and Paul, in Hart Minnesota. I then served part-time as Assistant Chaplain to the students and staff of The College of Saint Teresa in Winona for two years, and also part-time as financial director for the Immaculate Heart of Mary Seminary at St. Mary's College in Winona. Each of these experiences was a happy and challenging one. These various duties gave me confidence in my ability to work in different settings, and to do so effectively.

While Administrator at Sts. Peter and Paul, I had several most interesting experiences. One of them stands out in my memory. I was celebrating Mass one sunny spring morning for the thirteen farm families who made up the parish, when all at once, while I was preaching my sermon, there was a crash and a bang at the front door of the small church. Immediately next to the church was a smelly hog farm with poor fences, and following the noise, into the church marched a large, muddy, smelly sow, followed by ten of her brood.

Thank God there was an elderly hog farmer in attendance that Sunday. He spoke clearly, loudly and authoritatively, saying, "Parents, pick up your small kids. Nobody make a move toward the sow or her pigs. Sit quietly, don't speak, and don't move." That old farmer was a life saver that day. The sow and her offspring made their way slowly to the front of the church, spreading mud and manure on the way. When she found no food, she and her family turned and slowly exited.

That was probably the most exciting Mass ever celebrated in that little country church. Years later I met some people from that little community, and the first thing they said was, "Do you remember the day that the mother pig brought her ten little pigs into the church during Mass?" I told them that was indeed a "once in a lifetime" event that I would never forget.

The Dropped Ring

On another occasion, I was performing a wedding in that same little church. Immediately beneath the area in which the bride and groom stood to take their vows was a grill, beneath which was the furnace in a cave under the church. After the vows, as the groom was taking the ring from his best man to place on the finger of the bride, the ring fell through into the furnace below.

The farmer who served as superintendent of the church was present at the ceremony. He immediately ran out of the church and climbed down into a tunnel that led to the furnace. Miraculously, he found the ring in the ashes, wiped it off, and ran back upstairs. The wedding could go on! The couple is still married today, after 44 years, and I am certain that they have told their ring story hundreds of times by now, to the delight of their many listeners.

CHAPTER 8

A Couple of College of St. Teresa Stories

Subsequent to serving at the little Hart Church, I served as an Assistant Chaplain at the College of Saint Teresa in Winona on a part time basis. I offered the Mass daily and heard confessions several afternoons a week. *

I was returning to Winona on the evening of December 8th, 1969- the Feast of the Immaculate Conception. It was a bitterly cold night (10 below with a 5 mph wind blowing). As I drove through the campus, there suddenly appeared six young women in blue jeans, hitchhiking. Everything about this scenario

---

* I must say that through the experience of hearing confessions, I have been given a unique and intimate view of human nature that no other experience can provide. Vulnerable guilt in confessor as well as penitent sets the stage for growth, repentance, the owning of one's own destiny, and moving on in this beautiful, challenging experience called life- the life of a Christian.

was wrong: jeans were seriously against the dress code of the institution, and hitchhiking was absolutely forbidden. What is more, these girls were not dressed for the cold weather. I pulled my car over and the girls climbed in- four in the back seat and two in front with me.

From the back seat I heard, in a whispered tone, "My God- it's Father Nelson!" So, to sweeten the pot, I said to the riders, "Where are you going?" Silence for a second or two, and then from the back seat, "Where are *you* going?" I said I was going home, but I said they were obviously not dressed for the weather, and I would take them where they wanted to go.

I said again, "Where are you wanting to go? Please tell me and I will drive you there on this bitterly cold night." There was more whispering in the back seat, and then one of the girls said they were going across the bridge from Winona to Wisconsin, where they could drink legally. I said I would take them to the Black Horse Tavern in Wisconsin if that is where they really wanted to go.

The girls were a bit more comfortable with me by this time, and one of them said, "Would you come inside and let us buy you a beer?" I said to her, "My Dear, first of all, as a member of the faculty of the College of St. Teresa I have already broken the rule of not allowing students to wear blue jeans, and I have allowed you to hitchhike with me, which is also against the rules. The last thing I need now is to drink with under-aged students while acting as their chaplain." They excused me. I dropped them off at the tavern. End of story.

Here is another St. Teresa story : I received a call at the campus Chaplins' Home at about 10:45 PM one Friday night in early winter. The call was from a third year student who had returned to campus after an evening out with friends. She had been drinking, and she knew that the Sister monitoring the door would smell alcohol on her breath and expel her if she returned to her room via the normal route. Check-in time was 11:00, so she had no time to waste. She immediately called me to help her out of this critical situation.

Apparently she called me because I was a friend of her father. She explained her precarious situation, her total fear of being expelled from college, and her need for help. I asked her if she had a roommate she trusted, and she said she did. I invited her into the campus rectory and told her to call her roommate (no cell phones in those days!).

I also got on the phone with the roommate and told her about a window at the back of the dormitory. I told her how to unlock it, and asked her to be there to help me lift her roommate in through the window.

You see, my young friend was a good sized girl, and I was not sure I could boost her high enough to get her through the window on my own. So her roommate helped me get her in. We had to do it quietly, so as not to alert the Sisters. I told the girls that if they ever told on me, I could get into serious trouble.

She never ratted on me, and years later, when she was sending her own daughter off to college, she wrote to me, saying something like, "I hope she meets a rogue priest like you who can bail her out of troubles." I took that as a compliment.

More Job Moves

At the end of the 1971 school year, after just two years at St. Teresa, I was assigned to a different job. In addition to continuing my work at Cotter High School, I was to live at Immaculate Heart of Mary Seminary on the campus of St. Mary's University, and serve as financial officer for the seminary. I held that post until 1975. These were happy days, as the living situation was very comfortable. We had wonderful cooks- four Dominical Sisters from Switzerland. They baked bread every morning beginning at 4:00 AM. We all ate very well.

The staff of the seminary at that time was a team consisting of Fr. Robert Brom, Rector; Fr. Donald Schmitz, Spiritual Director; Monsignor Richard Feiten; and myself. We worked as part-time spiritual guides for the young men who were studying for the priesthood. I had loved the girls and the staff at St. Teresa College, and now was equally happy with the young men at the seminary. I was happy with my co-workers as well.

In the summer of 1975, diocesan policy concerning assignment term limits dictated that I had to move from Cotter, after having served as principal there for ten years. Bishop Loras Watters assigned me to serve as Superintendent of Catholic Schools for the Diocese of Winona, overseeing about fifty-five schools. I was also to serve as Principal of Loyola High School in Mankato, Minnesota. I agreed to try to fulfill this assignment.

After moving from Winona to Mankato I found myself living in a priests' building on the campus of the School Sisters of Notre Dame, Mankato Province. I asked Sister Ramona Schweich to assist me in the superintendence of the schools of the Diocese. Sister Ramona was a knowledgeable, competent and eager educator, and when she agreed to serve in that capacity my life was made much easier. Sister Ramona eventually took over the superintendence from me- a happy day! My one year of serving as superintendent of Diocesan Catholic Schools, and as Principal of Loyola High, a school of about 400 students, was a happy one.

CHAPTER 9

Airborne

My secretary that year at Loyola High School was Kay Hodapp, a very capable secretary and a wonderful human being. Her charity, respect and generosity were great examples for the students. Kay's husband Phillip was a member of the Minnesota Highway Patrol. One day at approximately 9:30 in the morning, Officer Phillip called me and told me that he and his partner, a pilot, were going to work the highways around Mankato from the air. Phillip wanted Kay, who had never been up in an airplane, to have the experience of flying. He asked me, "Would you be able and willing to go up in the plane with Kay and my partner for about an hour?" It was a quiet day around the school, so I said that I would be happy to join them.

When we were airborne, the pilot gave Kay and me stopwatches calibrated to indicate the speed of vehicles on the ground. We had great fun for the next hour tracking, timing, and having the pilot radio Phillip on the ground. We provided descriptions of vehicles and the speed at which they were traveling.

When we returned to the ground, the officers took Kay and me to lunch. I jokingly said to the two officers something like, "You guys are ruthless. Picking up speeders is like shooting fish in a barrel. It's too easy." Then I said to Phillip, "Surely you would not arrest your wife if you caught her speeding?" He countered immediately, "Oh yes I would. But I would arrange for her to have a pillow while in jail!" Another wonderful memory.

Back To Austin: Baseball, Fights and Flood

In April of 1976, I received a phone call from Bishop Watters at approximately 9:30 in the morning. I was working in my office at Loyola High School. He asked if I could see him around noon. I assured him that I could, and would be available to see him.

Bishop Watters came into my office, closed the door, and sat down. I recall thinking, "What did I do now, that he is unhappy about?" He took a deep breath and said something like, "Paul, I am going to ask you to move after just one year here in Mankato. You have done good work here, but we have a significant Diocesan problem. Pacelli High School is in legal trouble, with threatened lawsuits. It is in difficult circumstances, with people being divided, angry with each other, accusing each other, destroying unity in the church of Austin. I want to ask you to go to Austin, to be Principal of Pacelli and Coordinator of Catholic Education for the city, to try to lead the Church through this painful chapter. You know Austin, having been there before, and that should give you the best chance of helping the people there to resolve this crisis."

I remember saying to Bishop Watters, whom I respected and loved very much, "As a priest, the main thing I promised, when I was ordained into this diocese, was to obey the bishop in service to the people of my diocese, so my answer is that I will do my best to do what you ask." I was on my way to Austin in June of 1976.

I moved into Sacred Heart Hospice, a care center operated by the Sisters of St. Francis of Rochester, to assist the elderly chaplain, Father Earl "Quid" Byron, who was serving the patients living there. This was to be in addition to my duties in the Austin Catholic Schools. Quid received his nickname from the fact that as a younger man he had always asked a lot of questions, and the Latin word for "question" is "quid". He was bright, loving, interested in life, and generous. He taught me much as I assisted him, in small ways, to help others through the vulnerabilities of old age- failing health, fear, anxiety, and preparation for death. I learned here, on a daily basis, lessons in mortality, suffering, faith, and the courage to face the reality of our existence.

Quid was a Major League baseball fanatic. He knew the batting averages of players, past and present. And he knew team statistics; he could tell you who won the World Series in 1955. He was a walking baseball encyclopedia. Early in August, Fr. Quid was in failing health from Multiple Sclerosis (MS). He was very aware that he would not be strong enough to go to Twins games much longer. He said to me one day, "I surely would love to see the Twins play again." I told him that I would take him to a game any time he wanted to go.

A light went on in my head. I had a teacher working for me at Pacelli High School whose best friend was the second baseman for the Texas Rangers, and the Rangers were coming to Minneapolis the next week to play a series with the Twins. I called Bob, my teacher friend, and he called his friend in Texas. This young man sent us tickets located right behind home plate, about six rows up from the field. He also sent passes, so Fr. Quid and I could visit the Rangers dressing room before the game. Quid was overjoyed, and waited impatiently for the day to arrive.

When we met some of the players before the game, I remember how these young men were enthralled by the knowledge possessed by this shaking old priest. They stood listening in awe at his stories, as he recounted facts about baseball and its history. That was a memorable day for me, which I remember well after more than forty years.

I lived, and helped, in the Sacred Heart Hospice setting, but my main job was to address the pain, the divisiveness, the confusion, of the Catholic Schools of Austin. I approached this issue confidently, courageously, attentively, but also fearfully. I had walked into an angry place, space, moment, in the life of the Catholic Schools of Austin. Strong personalities had made their positions known.

The majority of the Catholic population of Austin, in my judgment, was not able or equipped to address the anger, the intensity of the moment. I soon learned, as I attempted to address this problem, that it would be bloody, public, confrontational, and difficult. But I had accepted the assignment, and remembering the courage of my parents when addressing the very heavy issues of their own lives, I dug in.

This was, without doubt, the most difficult, painful and impossible period of my life. The vast majority of the people of St. Augustine Parish, St. Edward Parish, and Queen of Angels Parish supported me in my efforts. But a small minority of people, mostly educated, wealthy, positioned, and in my opinion selfishly demanding, fought me to the end of my tenure in Austin on this, my second assignment there. Little did I know then that I would return to Austin, a place I loved, for a third term as priest and pastor.

I served as Principal of Pacelli for the next three years. In that third year, the Pastor of Queen of Angels Parish, Fr. Tom Ploof, resigned. Bishop Watters called me and asked if I would be interested in becoming Pastor of Queen of Angels Parish. I told him that, while I had enjoyed work, having been principal of three high schools over the previously fourteen years, I was ready to become a pastor.

Bishop Watters appointed me Pastor of Queen of Angels in the spring of 1977. I spent six most happy and wonderful years working with the people of the parish. My father died only a week after I took responsibility there, and the people of Queens were most supportive.

In my second year at Queen of Angels, the worst flood to hit Austin in over 100 years struck. It did significant damage to the church basement, the school dining hall, and some meeting rooms. The church basement had been a beautiful theatre, with padded seats bolted to the floor. All of this was destroyed by the flood waters, and the basement had to be gutted. The people of the parish rolled up their sleeves and did all of the work, removing the damage.

A good story: While the flood water was still in the large church basement, two young boys from the neighborhood came to me and asked if they could fish in it. I told the boys there were no fish there, just dirty water. The boys insisted they had seen fish down there. The stage was above the water level, so I told them to have their parents call me, and if the parents approved, the boys could fish. Within a few minutes the mothers called with their approval. The boys went to the basement, and within fifteen minutes came upstairs with five suckers, weighing about a pound each. One more time, the priest was not as smart as he thought he was!

In the summer of 1983, I was still scheduled to stay at Queen of Angels Parish for another two years, as the term of office at that time for pastors in our diocese was eight years. But on a Monday morning in early May, the phone rang for me. At the other end was my bishop, Loras Watters. We greeted each other, and then he asked me if I was planning to be in my office that morning. I told him I would be there, so he said he would see me at 11:00. That was all he said.

I spent the next two hours worrying, wondering what I had done, that he was coming to see me. The normal procedure is that when the bishop calls regarding an issue, a problem, or a possible change in assignments, the priest goes to Winona to see him, not the other way around! So I waited on pins and needles for the bishop to arrive at my door.

Bishop Watters arrived right on time, at exactly 11:00 AM. We sat, and he said something like, "Let's just get to the point. I know that you are very happy here, and that you are scheduled to stay here two more years, but I want you to seriously consider my proposal." Msgr. Robert Brom, the current Rector of the Cathedral in Winona, had just been named the Bishop-elect of the diocese in Duluth Minnesota. Bishop Watters wanted to assign me to take his place as Rector of the Cathedral, and also to reorganize the Catholic Schools of Winona. He warned me that reorganizing the finances of the city would be difficult work.

Winona had five parishes, four Catholic schools, and nine different salary schedules in their mix of institutions. There was also significant unhappiness in the ranks of the approximately 125 people working for the Church there, due to perceived inequalities in the pay schedules across institutions.

I told Bishop Watters for the second time that my only gift, promised at my ordination to the people of the diocese and to the bishop, was that I would obey orders. I said yes to the bishop's request, and my life was changed yet again- as history proves, for the better.

CHAPTER 10

On To Winona and the Cathedral

And so I moved again, from Austin to Winona, to begin life at the Cathedral of the Sacred Heart. Two associates, Fred Rolfstad and Tim Reker, lived with me at the rectory. Also living there were Fr. Cyril Fabian, a teacher of philosophy at St. Mary's University for more than thirty years, and Fr. John Daly, a retired priest of the diocese. We had a happy house and home together.

As the days went by, it appeared that matters in the parish were moving smoothly. The Catholic schools were financially very stressed, which also led to stress in the good people comprising their staffs. I invited the leaders of all five parishes, as well as the principals of the four Catholic schools, to come together to begin to address our common problems. This meeting took place at the Cathedral in the summer of 1983. During the next two years, more than 100 meetings of the various committees, boards and councils took place. I attended most of them, as did many other priests and parish and school leaders.

At the end of two years of respectful, intense, and sometimes uncomfortable dialogue, we, the Catholic leaders of Winona, agreed to conduct a major fund drive to raise money for the schools. We also established a new salary schedule that placed all Church employees on a fair and equitable scale. We had worked hard those two years, and there was great satisfaction in the fact that we had united the parishes, had a plan in place to correct the financial problems in the schools, and had hired a fund raising company to lead us in our plan to establish a Foundation for the Catholic Schools to the tune of at least a million dollars. Over the next year the Catholic people, as well as some non-Catholic friends, had pledged and contributed over $1,250,000 for the Catholic Schools of Winona. That effort, involving so many parish members from all the five parishes of Winona, brought back to life a very enthusiastic and hopeful spirit in the Winona Catholic Church.

The Death of My Brother's Wife

While I was serving as Rector of the Cathedral, a sad chapter unfolded in my family life and history.

My youngest brother Richard informed our family that his wife Linda was seriously ill with breast cancer. This was in early 1990, and as the weeks and months passed, Linda got very sick. She died on June 24, 1990. She left Richard with four children, girls aged ten and nine, and boys aged eight and six.

Linda died at home in St. Charles, Minnesota, at the Downtown Motel that Richard and she had operated for some time. Hospice people assisted Linda and Richard and their family during her death process.[*]

I officiated at Linda's funeral, and our family, as do all families who experience a death, moved on. Since the Cathedral was only twenty miles away from Richard and his children, I would take them one night a week, and let them stay overnight there, so that Richard could catch up on business and get some rest. The priests with whom I lived loved the kids, were very good to them, and didn't mind them running through the house, upstairs and down. Especially dear to the four kids was Fr. John Daly, a retired priest living at the Cathedral with me. He loved to tease the kids, chat and play with them, and they loved him.

---

[*] Hospice was then, and is now, a blessing to our society, in that it empowers people to deal with death, to participate in the dying process, and to face our universal mortality.

Things got pretty wild in the rectory sometimes, when he got the four of them going. Life, real life!

Beginning that summer, a month after Linda had died, I borrowed Richard's van and took his children on vacation for two weeks, to give him a break. He was a single parent raising four small children and also operating a motel in order to make a living for himself and them.

This first year we went west to the Black Hills and Yellowstone Park. For six years, the kids and I left home on the first of July and traveled through our country for two weeks. In those six years we visited forty-four of the forty-eight contiguous states in our nation. We had great fun, very little anxiety, frustration or anger with each other. The kids and I loved to travel and to see new things every day.

I enjoyed eight wonderful years at the Cathedral. I spent four years serving Bishop Watters, and four years working with Bishop John Vlazny. When they were in town, the bishops had dinner and evening prayer with us priests at the Cathedral rectory. This arrangement was for the most part a very enjoyable, interesting, and challenging experience. But there were moments of stress, as hierarchy and parish clergy discussed and debated the reality of church, as each camp saw that reality.

For a few of the eight years I spent as rector, I also directed the Newman Center at Winona State University and taught Theology at St. Mary's University for one semester. Young people from Winona State attended Mass at the Cathedral each weekend. This enriched our parish very much. The eight Cathedral years were hard work. I had to make challenging decisions, enjoyed enriching experiences, and happy days.

CHAPTER 11

Two Happy Years in Owatonna

After that eight year tour of duty (the term of office in the diocese at that time), Bishop Vlazny assigned me to serve as Pastor of St. Joseph Parish in Owatonna, Minnesota. I went there with a feeling of excitement, open to new challenges. St. Joseph showed itself to be a vibrant, open community, living the experience of the Gospel of our Christian faith. As I recall, there were roughly 1,100 families, or units, in the parish. It was open ecumenically to other denominations of Christian faith, and worked with agencies such as the Steele County Food Shelf, Steele County Hospice, and other social service organizations. I enjoyed every day of my life in Owatonna.

John and Betty

Shortly after arriving in Owatonna, I represented my parish at a Steele County Food Shelf meeting. I met several good people there, all concerned about the poor people in Steele County; but one member of the board stood out. He was quiet, eloquent, and insightful as to the mission, the philosophy, and the operation of the Steele County Food Shelf. He was Dr. John Arnesen, a retired Owatonna physician. I introduced myself to him and we became very close friends for the next seventeen years.

I visited John's home twice a month for breakfast, wonderful discussion, and laughter for those seventeen years until a few weeks before his death at the age of ninety-three. John had taken care of his wife, who was an Alzheimer's patient, in their home for ten years before she died, which was about a year before John himself died. His dear wife Betty was so affected by that painful disease that she did not know her husband of more than sixty years during the last months of her life.

John would let Betty wash the dishes after they ate a meal because she always had done so. She would not be able to get the dishes clean, but John allowed her to wash them anyway and place them in the cupboard. After she had gone to bed he would take the dishes out again and thoroughly re-wash them, replacing them again in the cupboard. Betty never knew that he did that. John was very patient, kind and loving toward his suffering wife. As I watched this process for over ten years, at least twice a month, I was deeply touched, moved, and changed. John Arnesen, a Buddhist, was one of my closest spiritual companions. I conducted funeral services for both Betty and John at an Anglican Church in Owatonna. The people who attended the memorial services got a kick out of the fact that a Catholic priest was praying in an Anglican Church for Buddhist people. I was honored beyond words to be a part of that experience.

We Establish a Foundation for Catholic Education in Owatonna

Shortly after arriving in Owatonna, I was told the people wanted to firm up support for their Catholic school, St. Mary's Elementary School. The Bishop of Winona and parish leaders in both parishes of Owatonna asked Fr. Harry Jewison, the Pastor of Sacred Heart Parish, and me, Pastor of St. Joseph Parish, to lead an effort to build a foundation for the Catholic school in Owatonna. We agreed to lead, and hired a firm to assist us in determining if we could raise significant funds. The firm did a preliminary study of the community and informed us that we could raise over a million dollars for the school. We organized the effort, placed parishioners in charge of the program, and went out to ask for pledges. Within three months, we surpassed our goal and renewed the spirit of generosity in the people of the town. At this writing, it is a big joy for me to know that the foundation is still helping students in Owatonna obtain a superb education.

Two happy years flew by for me as Pastor of St. Joseph. My brother priest, Harry Jewison at Sacred Heart, was also a good friend. We worked hard together and accomplished much in those two years. And then one morning in the late spring of 1993, I received a phone call from Bishop Vlazny asking if I would be in my office that day. I said that I would, and he told me that he would stop to speak to me around noon. Once again, I knew that something was up, as indeed it was.

Bishop Vlazny told me that he wanted me to return again to Austin, to become Pastor of St. Augustine Parish and Director of Austin Catholic Schools. This would be the third time I served in Austin. He indicated that there was turmoil at Pacelli High School, both legally and financially. He said that this issue was dividing the Church in Austin, and since I had been there twice before, he thought that I probably had the best chance of helping the people of Austin resolve this issue.

I said that I would go, but it was very difficult for me to leave Owatonna, as I was just beginning to feel as though I was at home there. I also knew that the climate in Austin would be electrified, to say the least. I packed my bags and headed the thirty-five miles south to Austin. This was in the summer of 1993.

CHAPTER 12

Back Once More In Austin

The next ten years were happy, and sometimes contentious, as I tried to work with the schools. I think, for the first time in my life as a priest, that I failed in my attempts to bring the community together, to resolve the Catholic School tension engendered by declining enrollments and financial stress on the parishes. The three parishes worked to do their best for the schools, while at the same time trying to be fair to all other aspects of Church life in the parishes.

Nonetheless, I loved every moment at St. Augustine Parish throughout the ten years. I was back to that parish a second time, as I had started there immediately after my ordination as a priest. The Parish Council and the Finance Council did great work in setting policies that enabled us to care for our people, in reaching out ecumenically, and in involving our people in the various aspects of the Austin community.

One painful period in my Austin pastorate came in the spring of 2000. I was in trouble with alcohol, and I was burned out. Bishop Harrington sent me to Saint Lake Institute in Silver Spring, Maryland for treatment, rest, and renewal in my priesthood. I was in treatment for six months. It was a painful, but a growing time. The people of St. Augustine Parish supported me all the way. This, plus the support of my family, enabled me to get through that difficult period.

At the end of my ten year term at St. Augustine in 2003 I was sixty-eight years of age. At that age, according to diocesan policy, priests could begin receiving the diocesan pension and retire if they chose to do so. I told Bishop Harrington (the Bishop of Winona at that time) that I had been heavy into Church administration for thirty-eight of my forty-two years as a priest. I had served as pastor of four of the largest parishes in the diocese: Queen of Angles in Austin, The Cathedral of the Sacred Heart in Winona, St. Joseph in Owatonna, and St. Augustine in Austin.

I was tired, and wanted out of the responsibility of directing, managing, financing, and growing these major institutions. I had loved what I was assigned to do for those forty-two years, and I was willing to continue to work, but would no longer be "the boss".

In 1999 I had built a small home in Rochester, and intended to retire there. I told Bishop Harrington that I would be open to serving as an Assistant Pastor in one of the Rochester churches. Within two days of that conversation, Bishop Harrington called me and asked if I would be Associate Pastor at St. Pius X Parish in northwest Rochester. I immediately and happily agreed to this assignment. At this moment, as I write these memoirs, I have been at St. Pius X Parish for eight years. I enjoy working with the great people of that parish and intend to continue to do so as long as I retain health of body, mind, and spirit.

SECTION III

ECUMENISM AND PUBLIC OUTREACH

CHAPTER 13

Ecumenism

Early in my priesthood I began to realize that we live in a multi-religious society, and that the people whom I served were involved with people of other religious traditions romantically, professionally, socially, educationally, and culturally. It has been a driving force within me to reach out to other religious traditions, continuously and openly. My extended family was of the Catholic and Lutheran traditions of Christian faith. I became aware that, in Minnesota, roughly forty percent of the citizenry is Catholic and another forty percent Lutheran. Marriages often are between a Catholic and someone of another Christian tradition (usually Lutheran or Methodist), or of a non-Christian tradition. Always, as young engaged couples came for marriage preparation, if they were involved in differing Christian traditions I invited the non-Catholic person to have his or her minister involved in the ceremony. Some chose to do this, others did not.

I have shared in the witnessing of marriages in Lutheran and Methodist churches many times. I have also hosted Lutheran and Methodist pastors in the Catholic church for marriages, funerals, and sometimes baptisms. My first ecumenical experience was on January 2, 1971, with a marriage between my former student Craig, a practicing Catholic, and his fiancé Dianne, who was a member of the Missouri Synod Lutheran Church, St. Martin's, in Winona. I participated at Dianne's Lutheran church with joy and gratitude that we were beginning to acknowledge each other, our differing traditions, and our differing approaches to the mystery of God, and our worship before God.

These experiences have always, I emphasize *always*, been most pastoral, most accepted, and promotional toward a mutual respect for each other's religious tradition. Christianity is slowly healed through this good will acceptance of differences in tradition, dogma and practice, as we worship our God, as we view our God together, without judgment as to whom we think is right or wrong theologically, historically, dogmatically. The Body of Christ is one, and has many members.

Twice in my life I participated in marriage ceremonies between a practicing Catholic and a Jewish fiancé. Each of the ceremonies was beautiful and moving for the participants and guests, and inspiring for the respective Rabbi and myself. Several times I have worked with couples, one of whom was Catholic and the other a member of a non-Christian tradition-Muslim, Buddhist, Hindu, and Native American.

While serving as Pastor of St. Augustine Parish in Austin from 1993 to 2003, I belonged to a pastoral group composed of leaders of congregations from the Lutheran, Methodist, Anglican, Congregational, and Roman Catholic traditions. All of us five were pastors. The group included one openly gay male pastor, a married female pastor, two married male pastors, and a celibate priest. We met every two weeks for coffee, discussion, community planning, serious and humorous dialogue. This was extremely rewarding, and it challenged me to crawl out of our Roman Catholic tendency to think that we are always right in dogmatic, moral, spiritual, and mystical positions. This experience taught me that each tradition of religious faith practice has beautiful traditions, contributions, movements, and emphasis to offer to the larger Church.

I belonged to, and was involved in, the ministerial associations of Austin, Winona, Mankato, and Owatonna, Minnesota for most of my fifty years as a priest. These were enriching, broadening, stretching experiences. Sometimes there was sadness, because one or another group of Christians excluded themselves from the larger group on moral, dogmatic, historical, or denominational issues.

Ecumenism has significantly come alive in the span of my lifetime. Since the Reformation in the Sixteenth Century, most denominations, including my own, were pretty much self-contained, self-satisfied, self-focused, and chose to demean traditions other than their own, rather than to affirm, respect, and encourage them as members of the Body of Christ. After Vatican II, our Catholic Church began to reach out, and many other Christian communities responded very favorably. Since the mid-1960's we have made significant progress in healing the pain, divisiveness, and separation of religious traditions, denominations and groups. It is a comforting conviction on my part, after almost fifty years as a priest, that Christian individuals, organizations, and denominations are much more aware of, open to, and willingly ready to work toward mutual respect, unity, and the realization that just as we differ nationally, culturally and socially, so we are different in our take on the religious structures, perceptions, convictions and positions of life in the world. We all possess the Spirit of God in us, we all are imperfect, and we all have a contribution to make to the whole. This is historical, slow progress.

Community Involvement and
Noli Carborundum Illegitimi Sunt

Another dimension of life that has touched the depths of my mind, spirit and soul was the involvement in civic, professional, and social outreach programs in the various communities in which I lived. In my first assignment in Austin, Fr. Tighe, my principal, asked me to serve as the Athletic Director of Pacelli High School. This enabled me to negotiate from time to time with the local Austin Public School System in the sharing of their football field and their gymnasiums. The costs, supervision, and responsibilities of both the public and the Catholic schools had to be taken into consideration. This was the first experience for me as a priest and a professional in this sort of civic responsibility. I always very much enjoyed my work with public school administrators, athletic directors, coaches, and other involved persons. This experience taught me, at a young age, to deal with, share with, and negotiate with people who had a different take on reality than I did. So my first assignment in Austin as a priest was most formative, informative, and foundational for my life.

As I mentioned previously in these pages, after three years in Austin, Bishop Fitzgerald assigned me to serve in Winona, part-time teaching at Cotter High School, part-time serving as Assistant Director of Religious Education for the Diocese of Winona, and part-time serving as an Assistant Pastor at St. John's Parish in Winona. This was a happy year. By the end of the spring of 1965 I had finished my Masters Degree in Educational Administration at St. Mary's University, and Bishop Fitzgerald assigned me the responsibility of being the Principal of Cotter High School. This meant managing more than 600 students, and more than 50 full and part-time staff members.

As I stepped into the responsibility of Principal of Cotter, I was invited to join the Winona Exchange Club, a service organization that works at making its members grow, and serving the local community's needs. I joined, was active in the club for ten years, served as its president one year, and truly became a citizen of the Winona community through this wonderful experience and involvement.

Belonging to the Exchange Club from 1965 to 1975 enabled me to meet many wonderful men, and later, as we broke through the sexist exclusiveness, women. The dropping of the men-only membership was a happy, and for most of the membership, an easy transition.

One of the men whom I met and became good friends with was a lawyer by the name of Bob Hull.

He belonged to the Congregational Church of Winona. After a couple of years, he invited me to come
to his church and speak about Roman Catholicism. I
told him that I was honored to speak on this issue, but
that I expected the Congregational people to also in-
struct and inform me as to their beliefs, emphasis, and
spirituality. This happened, and a new relationship between significantly different traditions developed,
strengthening the future of ecumenism in Winona.
Both Bob and I felt good about this development.

Within a year or two of my speaking to the
people of his church, Bob's wife, whom he loved
dearly, was stricken with a very debilitating disease
that kept her bedridden for more than two years. She
was suffering, not only from her physical disease, but
also from a significant depression.

One day as Bob and I were having lunch, I told
him a story. The story was about people picking on
other people less able to defend themselves. And as
the story unfolds, it brings in a priest of the early
twentieth century, and thus a man who knew the Latin
language. The priest said to the victims in Latin, *Noli
carborundum illegitimi sunt,* which translated into
English means, "Don't let the bastards get you down."

Bob asked if he could make a plaque of that
saying for his wife. I said "No!" I wanted to have the
plaque made for her, and so I did. When I gave them

the plaque, Bob hung it on the wall at the foot of his wife's bed, and he told me that for years to come the plaque did more for his wife's healing process than did anything else, because when her friends came to visit they would ask her what it meant. She would tell her guests, laughter would ensue, and then the guests would invariably ask, "Where did you get that?" and she would laughingly say, "From a Catholic priest." My friend Bob said that he and his wife had more laughs and fun over that simple plaque than from any other aspect of her recovery. I learned again that we need to laugh, to not take ourselves too seriously.

CHAPTER 14

The Mission of the Catholic Schools

When I took over as Principal and leader of Cotter High School I was thirty years old, and very inexperienced in leading, managing, and helping people. I asked my predecessor, Fr. Jim McCauley, "What is the most important behavior for me, so that I may provide fair, effective, and positive discipline, especially with students, but also with staff members?" Jim immediately responded, "Learn and memorize each person's name. If you can call them by name, you will be effective." That is, perhaps, the most powerful piece of advice I ever received at that young age. Jim was right. I began to memorize names every summer, and for the most part, I was very successful in leading three different high schools: Winona Cotter for ten years, Mankato Loyola for one brief year, and Austin Pacelli for three years. These were profoundly happy years, as I dealt with the young people and the amazing staff in all three schools. In the sixties and seventies staff people were paid minimally, and in retrospect very unjustly; but they were men and women who gave their lives to the students-not for monetary gain, but for the joy of forming young lives.

I am convinced that the great success of the Catholic schools in this country, from the earliest days of the immigrants coming to America, was due to the fact that the people in the classrooms had a mission. The mission was to inform, to inspire, and to empower the students they taught, in order to set them on a course of personal progress. The Religious women and men of the Catholic Church laid the foundation for American education through their methods of inspiring, challenging, and motivating their students. American education today is the child of the Catholic Religious men and women who devoted their lives to educating the children of the poor immigrants, discovering what was effective, inspiring, and challenging to the young people who sat before them in the classrooms. Those teachers were not afraid to challenge each student, to push the student to the brink, even if the child might report that challenge to his or her parents. The formula, in that time frame, worked, because parents somehow knew that if their children did not get a good education, a happy life was lost to them.

Spiritual Leadership

Spiritual development for the people I have dealt with seems to rest on qualities of relationship: the relationships between people and the mystery of God, between people in general, between the people with responsibilities in social organizations and those participating in those organizations. In my experience, authentic and honest communion and communication comprise the bedrock for organizational effectiveness, organizational peace and happiness, organizational efficiency and success.

Spiritual leadership is a profound challenge, a beautiful opportunity, a humbling journey. To be a spiritual leader, it has appeared to me, involves the continuing growth in the spirit of communion with the mystery of God, self, others, and all of creation; emotional and social maturation of the leader; the continuing intellectual development of the leader; and the continuing willingness of the leader to address and participate in the most challenging and difficult moments of social interaction.

Spiritual leadership also demands reflection, prayer, the willingness on the part of the leader to own the entirety of his or her being. Humility, meaning "knowing one's place and taking it", is an essential piece of the puzzle needed to effectively help and lead

an organization as it grows peacefully and meaningfully. A spiritual leader must continuously work at integrity of mind, peace of soul, calmness of spirit, balance of emotion and passion, determination of intention, generosity of energy (which means that one
works long hours, without becoming a victim).

Spiritual leadership has to flow from the heart,
mind, and person of one who knows and owns his or
her limits, weaknesses, prejudices, negative habits. A
good spiritual leader has taken his or her own inven-
tory thoroughly, honestly, frequently. As a Roman
Catholic priest, I have had access to the Sacrament of
Reconciliation all of my life. This is the sacramental
experience, when a person approaches a priest-
confessor and confesses to God and to the priest, who
represents Jesus and the Christian community, the ex-
act nature of his sins, failings and selfishness. This has
been, for me, very challenging for my entire life. I
don't mind telling anyone of my successes. I fear telling anyone of my weaknesses, sins, faults, compro-
mises with the Gospel call. In the seminary we went
to confession weekly. As we left the seminary, we
were advised to acquire a spiritual director, to discipline ourselves to prayer several times a day, and to
celebrate the Sacrament of Confession at least once a
month. With very few exceptions, I have kept my feet
to the fire, insisting that I approach a confessor once a

month. This discipline has enabled me to come back, again and again, to the spirit of Jesus Christ. Humility, accurate self-knowledge and self acceptance, are essential to spiritual leadership.

Leadership demands, if it is to be effective, life-giving and successful, that the leader have intellectual awareness, emotional stability, personal maturity, the social graces, and a readiness to change, adjust, reset the course of the preplanned journey. Spiritual leadership demands bringing the mind home to the present moment, and staying in the present moment of reality and life.

Spiritual leadership involves communication, listening attentively, and speaking prudently, briefly, and meaningfully to those persons in one's charge; and being emotionally and spiritually accepting to others, available to others, and always respectful of others. This is no small challenge. Personal opinions, religious, political, social convictions, our prejudices, our personal insecurities, can so easily destroy the tone, the atmosphere, the settings, that will enhance and enable good communication, trust, and openness to work together. This burden, while not totally that of the leader, rests mostly on the leader's attitudes and approaches, and is the responsibility of spiritual leadership.

As of this writing, I am approaching fifty years as a priest. While I know that I have made gains in the disciplines and practices of spiritual leadership, I am continually made aware that to be a spiritual leader, discipline, awareness, and presence of mind and attention are essential needs in any encounter with another person. Authentic spirituality is the opening, the invitation, the availability of the spiritual leader for those with whom he or she works. If one is real, humble, able to listen, and has a history of accepting people, then others will trust enough to approach with their vulnerability, their secrets, their shame, their guilt and fear. It is my conviction that the greatest gift that a spiritual leader can make available to others is a trusted, authentic self-knowledge and self-acceptance which deliver stability, a realistic humility, an openness of confidence, and the gentle acceptance of the person who chooses to approach. Self-image and peace of mind empower a spiritual leader, such as a parent, a teacher, a priest, a minister, a rabbi; a social leader of any significance, such as a scout leader, a 4-H leader, to be the energy, the insight, the inspiration for those with whom they work.

In my estimation, people who end up in vocations that touch, immediately and intimately, the lives of their constituents, have a unique opportunity to inspire and move their children, their students, their patients, their participants, into growth that mere cognition and intellection cannot make happen. Part of the human brain and soul participates in cognition and informational thinking; and part of the human soul participates in appreciating, pondering and reflecting. The spiritual leader must touch the latter dimension of human beings. This is the work of religion, spirituality, community, and humanitarian unity and growth.

Almost every day of the fifty years I have spent living as a priest out and among people, I have been approached with human suffering, human fear, human defeat, human divisions, human emotions and passions- in the corners of stores, in jails and prisons, on street corners. I have been approached on airplanes, in foreign lands, in death scenes, and at wedding receptions. I have been invited to lunch or dinner when the person felt secure in approaching the priest, the mystical representative of God and the community, in search of peace, relief, comfort. People have come seeking relief of pain in almost any conceivable setting. This is one of the greatest privileges, comforts and opportunities of my priesthood.

Human suffering, pain, fear and despair bring us together. I have learned, over all the years, that one of the greatest gifts that a priest can give is to listen attentively to the person, the penitent, the suffering individual, as they make every effort to deal with their pain, insecurity, fear, guilt and shame. Guilt and shame lock us down, and steal years of peace from many of us, until we achieve a point of view in which we can face ourselves. Only then can we face another, and then we can find peace. Sigmund Freud, who was not a religious man, is reported to have said over a hundred years ago that the Roman Catholic practice of confession is the most widespread and effective reliever of psychiatric pain known to modern psychology and medicine.

Many people who come to speak about their issue, whatever it may be, have carried it for ten, thirty, fifty, or more years. Almost always, when they have disclosed their sin, guilt, shame, secret, failure, they cry and acknowledge that they feel new life, forgiveness, acceptance, and peace. One of the truly powerful gifts of the Roman Catholic tradition of faith is the Sacrament of Reconciliation because it enables Catholic (and other denominational Christians) to confess guilt, realize hope, and find new life.

Some years ago I attended a conference in Minneapolis on acquiring, maintaining, and living in and with mental and spiritual peace. The presenter was a psychiatrist, whose name I cannot remember. He was a dynamic man, an excellent and humorous speaker, and had an amazing stage presence that kept his audience engaged through several talks from 8:00

AM to 5:00 PM. A gesture, which he used perhaps fifty times that day, was to raise his hands high above his head, sweeping the hands, palms always facing forward, behind his back, and then lowering his hands to below his waist and bringing them forward, saying as he did so, "You must bring the whole of your life with you. I repeat, if you want peace of mind, you must bring the entirety of your life with you." He explained that by that repeated gesture and message, he was impressing on us, his listeners, that to find peace of mind, comfort of conscience, peace of soul, each person had to own the entirety of his or her life. Each person must deal with guilt, shame, defeat and failure. It is owning this dimension of our experience that we can move on, find our dignity, accept forgiveness, and live in peace. This is basically the theology, psychology, and spirituality of the Catholic Sacrament of Reconciliation.

CHAPTER 15

Our Cemeteries and Cemetery Boards

Another area of life, important to the vast majority of people, is the way in which they remember their deceased loved ones. Catholics generally are very proud of their cemeteries. They visit the cemeteries, wherein the bodies of their loved ones are placed, either in a grave or in a columbarium (which usually contains the cremates of the deceased, although bodies in caskets may also be placed in the columbarium). It follows, then, that the cemetery must be maintained beautifully, carefully, reverently.

I served on the Austin Catholic Cemetery Board for sixteen years, the Winona Catholic Cemetery Board for eight years, and the Owatonna Catholic Cemetery Board for two years. Twenty-six years of monthly meetings of cemetery boards taught me many profound lessons. To finance the cemetery is always a challenge, trying to keep the costs affordable for all people. To plan long-range goals, and to learn to be very patient with families, most of whom have dealings with the cemetery only when a family member has died, is also a challenge. Families are often stressed, mourning, uninformed, vulnerable, and sometimes confused and bewildered emotionally.

We remember peak moments in our lives, usually quite graphically. The death of a family member is such a moment, and focuses our attention very clearly on what is happening, how the management and assistance of the church, the clergy and the assistants unfolds. So there must be a spirit of compassion and patience, and a clear education as to the realities, the procedures, and the total experience of burying the dead of the respective families.

Cemetery boards deal with all this and more. A big responsibility of the leadership of cemetery boards is to continuously educate, inspire, and empower the other board members with a tangible sense of compassion and patience with people at the time of death. While the cemetery is a business, and needs to be managed responsibly, it is also the stage which touches people at their most vulnerable, emotional, and perhaps confused moments.

There is usually at least one strong-willed member of every cemetery board who just wants to get the job done, efficiently and in a financially safe manner, and get on to the next problem. Many times in my pastoral role on these boards, I learned to hold my tongue, to advise quietly and calmly, to hold to the reality of gentleness for the board members and for the families we serve at the death of their loved one. Cemetery boards were many times for me humbling classrooms. On the other hand, cemetery work and management brought me much satisfaction, peace and happiness.

Most years on Memorial Day, if the weather cooperated, I was privileged to celebrate Mass at the local cemeteries in Austin, Winona and Owatonna. Hundreds of people would show up for the Mass, and then spend time visiting their respective graves. People would come in wheelchairs, on crutches, with the assistance of family members or friends. Young people would come to visit the graves of their dead. Always there was a spirit of deep respect present in the gathered congregation. Always it seemed people were more ready and willing to show their tears, their grief, their loss; and people mourned quietly and openly for their loved ones.

Each year during my pastorate in Austin I would arrange for parents, usually the mothers, to drive fourth and fifth grade students to our cemetery. When we arrived at the cemetery I would speak briefly about the sacredness of our burial grounds, and then would allow the students to wander around the cemetery, seeking the graves of their loved ones, or of people they had known. I also gave them pads of paper and pencils so that they could record the oldest dates they would find on the tomb stones.

The cemetery visit for these ten and eleven year old children always ended at the section of the cemetery in which the infants were buried. This seemed to be the most profound moment for these children, as they found the name of a baby of whom they had heard, or the baby of a family they knew, or sometimes of their own baby brother or sister. The parents were always very touched by the demeanor, the attitude, the reverence of the children, as they experienced the cemetery. Death is a mystery, a truth, a reality which touches all of life, and yet defies all of life to comprehend it. It insists that we simply participate in its reality.

Mysteries surround us. One mystery is our home, the universe in which we live and of which we are a part. Mysteries are truths which are real, incomprehensible, astounding, inspiring, frightening. These mysterious truths grip the entirety of our being, of our imagination, of our ability to be open and inspired, to be vulnerable and afraid, and to be conscious and totally dependent on forces and energies which are far beyond us.

Many young people in high school have experienced death. Early in my priesthood I became aware of this as I dealt with families of the dying. In all of the communities in which I served as pastor, I contacted the local mortuary and asked if we could bring our young people to them for a tour and an explanation of what happens when a death occurs. I found all of the morticians to be most helpful, and I always found that the young people were most interested, intrigued, and focused on the explanation of the process of preparing a body after death for a respectful and dignified experience for the family and friends. Young people were very engaged in these experiences, and would express their gratitude to us for having arranged the tour.

CHAPTER 16

The Tragedy of Suicide

While I served as pastor of St. Augustine Parish in Austin from 1993 to 2003, Mower County, of which the city of Austin is a part, experienced the suicides of eleven young people during a fifteen month period of time. The victims were from fifteen to thirty-three years of age. The majority of them were involved in my ministry in one way or another. I held six of the funerals and was deeply involved with the families as they worked their way through these horribly painful times of loss, grief, and searching.

The intense pain and fear that accompanied this rash of suicidal deaths of the youngsters reverberated through the city of Austin, and throughout the county. I asked Bobbi Greenly, a former student of mine at Pacelli High School, to help me form and lead a support group for the family and friends of suicide victims in the Mower County area. She graciously and enthusiastically agreed to do so. Bobbi's own son, a twenty year old, had been one of the victims. She was an inspiration to many as she dealt with her own pain and at the same time empowered others to deal with theirs.

We began to hold support meetings for the family members and friends of people who had taken their own lives at the St. Augustine parish rectory in 1995. The meetings continued for several years. We had people from all over southeastern Minnesota coming to these meetings. People who had experienced the pain of suicide supported each other through prayer and shared stories. They cried together, and found new meaning and hope for their deceased loved ones and for themselves. I learned through this experience that the greatest healer of deep and intractable emotional pain is the opportunity to share it with others who have had similar experiences. The healing power of the community was always obviously present in these meetings.

As a byproduct of these experiences, a panel was formed consisting of myself, a minister, a social worker, and a parent who had lost a child to suicide. We televised a show on the local public television channel addressing the issues of suicide, depression, the need to seek help, and the need to share pain in families, schools, churches, and with friends. We also developed a simple flier that we distributed to all of the schools in Mower County. We distributed enough of these so that every educator and every student would have one. This was an effort by the community to try to help resolve this painful experience for the entire population of Mower County. Obviously, it is impossible to know how, or if, this effort helped, but it was a sincere effort to address a painful, frightening, and very serious problem among our young people.

While I served as Principal of Pacelli High School in Austin, during the 1976 school year, I had to discipline one of the junior boys. He was a very unhappy and angry young man, and that attitude usually got him into trouble in the classroom, in the halls, and during lunch hour. He experienced conflicts with teachers and peers. On the day of which I speak, I assigned him to report to detention after school. This was a supervised study hour in the school, beginning immediately after school was dismissed. It was for students who were having difficulty academically, socially, behaviorally, or relationally. He chose to ignore the detention. I tried to stop him as he left school, telling him that ignoring this discipline would only lead to more severe punishment.

He ignored my advice, went home, and called his little brother into the bathroom. When the younger brother got there, he put a gun in his mouth and killed himself there, in his brother's presence. This traumatized the family horribly of course, and the young boy

who witnessed this terrible act had difficulty emotionally for years.

I officiated at the boy's funeral, counseled his
family for years, and experienced some emotional difficulty myself, wondering if I could have handled the
situation better, differently, more prudently. This was
one of the most difficult and sad experiences of my
entire life as a priest. Since that experience, every
time I have been called to a suicide scene, an image of
that boy and his brother and family forces itself into
my mind. The horrors of emotional disease, and of all
the human attitudes, emotional states, depressive and
chemical issues that lead to suicide are such a huge
mystery to our culture yet, that I am humbly stopped
in my tracks, acknowledging that I know very little
about this painful dimension of our society.

We immediately react to the symptoms of significant physical illness. These conditions seem to be
more measurable, more manageable, and more solv-
able than do the mental, emotional, sociological and
spiritual issues in our lives. Our culture, in my experience, has the need to delve deeper into human reality,
human pain, the human ability and willingness to deal
with these issues.

It is comparatively easy to diagnose appendici-
tis, heart disease, neuropathies, and most other physical illnesses. But it is extremely difficult to recognize

and deal with psychological, emotional, and spiritual issues. They seem to be very difficult to accept, to address, to discuss, and to process, for individuals, families, and social institutions.

It strikes me, through experience listening to confessions, listening to pain expressed in my office, feeling the tensions in homes, that one of the greatest lacks in our modern culture is the willingness, the ability, the developed discipline needed to listen sincerely and attentively to another person, especially in emotionally charged moments and experiences of life. Jesus taught that we should pray constantly, and that command is really that we should listen constantly to the person who is present to us at any given moment. Being overwhelmed with speed, efficiency, activity, business, distractions, noise, music, cell phones, and other modern instruments of immediate communication, can rob us of the power of person. The experience of authentic communion is wounded, and in many cases killed, and this reality is taking its toll on the health of our modern culture.

CHAPTER 17

My Home in Rochester

As I mentioned previously in these pages, when I approached sixty-eight years of age in 2003, I had been a priest for forty-two years. I was tired of responsibility, of stress, of financial management, of parish disputes, of overseeing the physical plants, the people, and the energy of a parish. I had planned to retire in Rochester since I had served in Austin, Winona, Mankato and Owatonna. I wanted to retire where I would not be known as much as a priest. Also, my family lived in the Rochester area, and I wanted to be a part of their lives, as best I could, in my retirement years. My brothers and their families had been so supportive of my life, different as it was, and I wanted to share my life with them as well, and as frequently, as I could.

This being the case, I contracted the Dewitz Construction Company in 1999 to build me a small house in northwest Rochester. The house is small, easy to clean, and very functional for me and Salley, my wonderful poodle dog. I have a wonderful view. I can see Eyota, fifteen miles away to the east, from my deck. I can also see the horizon of the northern hemisphere for three to ten miles. I am a visual person and so consider this living setting a profound blessing because every day I stand and look in awe at the horizon north of me. God's creation comes alive every day for me in the changes, in the fertility, in the stability of life that I see before me.

Having grown up on a farm, I love the view of fields through the seasons. I enjoy watching the calves being born on the hillside in the spring, the tractors planting, and later harvesting, the crops. I look to the northeast and see the Franciscan Sisters' Mother House nestled on the hill, and I am reminded daily that the Franciscan Sisters educated me and gave me an appreciation of and for life that has been rich, interesting, and challenging. The Sisters of St. Francis have been a powerful presence in the development of Rochester, and they have educated thousands of southern Minnesota children who grew into powerful citizens, helping to develop our society in this area.

Seeing God's creation as a way of life has sustained me. To realize daily that God is present in modes, in patterns, in energies, in movements, in developments, in changes, in productivity, in unpredictable presentations, and in more categories than the human mind can describe, is a prayer for me. This energy opens my mind to possibility, my heart to inclusivity, and my soul to mystery.

To listen to the sounds of silence of God's creation, to feel the distances of the horizon through my perception, to realize the immensity of God's gifts, is, and has been, a source of meditation, contemplation, appreciation, and wonder for me throughout the years that I have been privileged to live at this location. Living here, with the vision I have experienced day and night is a renewing realization that my second skin, that is, the setting within which I live, is as essential to my happiness, my peace of mind, my calmness, my mental, spiritual and emotional health, as is my very being alive.

Saint Pius X Parish

I have had eight wonderful years at St. Pius X Parish. I work with people who want to live the Gospel message with and for each other. I am also privileged to visit the Rochester hospitals several times a week, to serve at least eight rest homes frequently, and to say Mass at many of them from time to time. One of the gifts of being and serving as a priest is that I am reminded frequently of how lucky I am to be able, at my current age of seventy-six, to walk into and out of rest homes in which I visit patients younger than myself. How rewarding and humbling my work has been, and continues to be.

St. Pius X Parish is a home for, and of, humble people who work together to serve the needs and to comfort the pains of families and individuals in our parish and beyond. People from the parish serve the local community, visit the rest homes and hospitals of our community, visit the elderly sick and shut-ins of our parish, work at the jail and the local state prison, assist the Dorothy Day Home for the homeless, and work to comfort the patients at the Cronin House, which is a home for the chronically chemically ill.

St. Pius Parish has members who serve on hospice boards, to assist people who are dying. We are honored by a member of the parish, Dick Dale, who never seeks recognition, but who was recently named Minnesota Hospice Volunteer of the Year.

I appreciate Dick's award, because he and our mutual good friend Don Carlson, a retired FBI agent, visited my mother's farm home at Christmas with a plate of cookies the year before she died at 99- plus years of age. I happened to be home when they came, and knowing each of these guys, as I let them in the door I said, "Ma, watch what you say because the cops and the FBI are here!" After Dick and Don left our home, my mother scolded me, telling me, her seventy-two year old son, that I should not be disrespectful of people who were coming to be kind. I uncharacteristically kept my mouth shut, but I have told Dick and Don the story, which they enjoyed greatly.

As I live in the St. Pius community and watch them reach out to and serve the various dimensions of society, I am deeply touched. Every day there are people from the parish who, with no desire to be recognized, serve in liturgical and service activities that inspire, comfort, and lead others to enjoy life the best they can. This is living the Gospel.

CHAPTER 18

The Church

When I was ordained to the priesthood almost fifty years ago, the priest was king, dictator, boss, the guy who said what was going to happen, like it or not. In the sixties all of that changed, and in my opinion, "Thank God!"

Life was a bumpy road, church-wise, for the next few years, from 1961 through 1964. The Church was converted from the Latin Rite to the responsibility of being a Church that understood the vernacular, literally throughout the world, in several hundred dialects and languages.

Vatican II was a peak moment in the history of the Catholic Church, and in the Christian Church throughout the world. That experience called all believing Christians to reexamine their beliefs, their practices, and their expectations of the Gospel and their willingness and readiness to live the Gospel. We were also asked to look at how we saw each other, as believers, as protestors, and as divided groups of believers.

Church history speaks of the human journey through the eyes of Church people. A friend, Dr. John Graner, taught me a profound lesson, when he said one day, "History is always written by the winners." How true that is, and what an insight to embrace, because it teaches us to read, to research, to investigate critically and thoroughly any issue, any relationship, any involvement that affects our lives.

Life in the Church has always been restless, imperfect, confused, and managed because Church is people, and people are restless, imperfect, confused, and managed. The history of the Church for the last seventy-five years has included me. I have experienced in that Church inspiration, beauty, hope, community, transcendence, mystery, forgiveness, love, and a host of other positive qualities. I have also experienced, in those seventy-five years of Church, doubt, betrayal, dishonesty, clerical manipulation of people, hierarchical cover-up of horrible abuses including, but not limited to, sexual abuses, financial abuses, and structural abuses.

The Church is a wonderful communion of people, and the Church is also a political structure. As in civil government, the Church leaders want to show their best side, downplay problematic issues, and secure power from their vantage point. Institutions, civic, religious and social, must manage their affairs in such a way that they sustain their structure and keep their leaders in control. Governments and churches get into trouble when managerial secrecy, limited consultation on issues of broad interest, and a tendency to restrict contact and conversation only to the "inside" group- leadership's chosen advisers- is the plan of governance. Sadly, it has been my experience that this is the reality in Church politics, management, and delivery systems throughout my proud fifty years of being an integral part of the Catholic Church in the Diocese of Winona.

Granted that much good has been achieved, many services have been delivered, and many people have been well served in the Church of Winona. That is a beautiful gift to culture and society. But the fact remains that cover-ups have occurred, and people who have been the victims of sexual abuse have been betrayed and dismissed when they threatened the structure of the Church. The fact of the matter also is that millions of Catholics in the United States have left our communion over the past thirty years. Our Church structures have had to sell off property in order to pay for law suits. Many parishes have been closed in the United States, partly due to population shifts, but also partly because Catholics have walked away from our religious tradition.

As Catholics we must, in my opinion, continuously examine our practices, our ecclesial and social power application, our leadership attitudes and practices, our Gospel authenticity, our communion with the larger Church and society. We must ask ourselves frequently just why people are leaving our communion, why our financial support is falling off, why our social and political influence is diminishing. Negative results have always been, for me, difficult to examine, and yet, to keep my balance, I know that I must assess the negative aspects of my being, not just the positive and pleasant dimensions of life.

Our Church structure has, in my observation, turned a blind eye to the full dimensions of our strengths, our weaknesses, our potential, and our challenge. People do not leave an institution that serves them well, but millions are leaving the Church in the United States. It would seem that we, the leaders of the faith tradition, must look closely and critically at every aspect of our being.

1. Great-grandmother Nelson.

2. My grandparents: Mary & John O'Connell, Peter & Elizabeth Nelson.

3. My parents' wedding picture. Left: My father Claude & my mother Lenora. Right: My dad's brother Ervin (Bud) & my mother's sister Ruth. Photo taken June 5, 1934.

146

4. Mother's family. Left to right: Florence, Grandma O'Connell, Lenora (my mother), Gertrude, Ruth.

5. Father's family. Left to right: Back row: Ida, Lillian (Curly), Margaret (Mutt), Violet (Blondie). Front row: Irvin (Bud), Theodore (Ted), Claude (my father).

6. My mother and me in 1935.
Nice hat, Ma!

7. My godmother Gert and me
in 1935.

8. Me at age two. Tough guy!

9. The farmhouse in which I grew up, Simpson, MN.

10. St. Bridget's Church, established in 1859. My home parish.

11. My First Communion class in 1942: front row, far left.

12. Showing an Angus bull for 4-H, age 13.

13.My Confirmation class in 1945: right front.

14. College graduation photo, 1957.

15. St. Paul Seminary Jazz Band, 1958: trombone second from right.

16. Ordination picture, 1961.

17. My friend Charles Quinn and me at St. Augustine's, 1961.

18. Mother, Dad & me at my first Mass dinner, 5/31/61.

19. Joe DiMaggio & me in
Minneapolis, spring 1969.

20. Me playing in a basketball game fund raiser, Loyola High School, 1976.

21. My brothers Richard and Bernard & my mother and me, 2004.

22. Austin Human Rights Award, 2004.

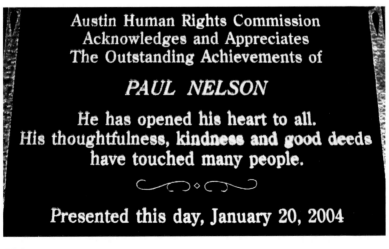

Austin Human Rights Commission
Acknowledges and Appreciates
The Outstanding Achievements of

PAUL NELSON

He has opened his heart to all.
His thoughtfulness, kindness and good deeds
have touched many people.

Presented this day, January 20, 2004

23. Myself and my dear friends and house mates, Salley and Dusty, 2005.

SECTION IV

REFLECTIONS ON THE SACRAMENTS

CHAPTER 19

The Sacraments

Sacramental ministry is a tremendously important aspect of Catholicism, especially for Catholic priests. Every sacrament that is celebrated is recorded in official books at each Catholic church throughout the world. We Catholics observe and celebrate seven sacraments: Baptism, Confirmation, Reconciliation (confession), Eucharist, Marriage, Holy Orders, and Anointing of the Sick. Many times in Catholic practice, a person is required to obtain an updated version of his or her baptismal certificate as, for example, before marriage, before confirmation, before First Eucharist. Thus, a great emphasis is placed on good and accurate record keeping.

People often return to the community in which they grew up, to their childhood parish church, in order to find their roots. They are interested in the marriage of their parents, the histories of their grandparents, the dates they received the sacraments, and other personal history. I have come to know that this is a very important work of the structural Church, to keep accurate records. People need them to go back to, in order to understand their lives.

Sacraments are not about individuals. Sacraments, as they are understood, appreciated, and applied in the Roman Catholic Church tradition, always involve the community. When a child is baptized the entire family changes. When a young person is confirmed, the family takes a step deeper into life, faith and mystery. When a member of the family goes to confession seeking reconciliation, the emotional, spiritual, and social atmosphere of the family is altered. As members of the family share in the Eucharist, all are reminded that charity is the way of life, as taught by Jesus, and that life is the essence of existence in the Christian setting.

Marriage

As people assume the responsibility of marriage, fidelity is promised, a stable setting is put into place for the arrival of children, and for their quiet, stable, and continued development. Two people become one, in willingness, in effort, in patience, in mutual respect and forgiveness, in a vision, and in all that it takes to make these dimensions of life happen. Society is gifted, renewed, and stabilized as two people commit to each other in the public celebration of love, respect, communion, and commitment.

Marriage is a sacrament because it consecrates the two individuals to each other, and it is a visible gift to the larger community. It is the root of social stability, the foundation needed for peace in the family, in the community, in larger society, in the world. Marriage touches the entirety of life. It blesses the children born into the family unit to hope, security, and to a vision for the unfolding of their own lives and destinies. Marriage is a sacrament because marriage is generative of life, not just sexually, biologically and anatomically, but marriage is the basic contributor to society, marriage is the foundation for stability, marriage is the vision needed for peace, happiness, and security in individuals and in the culture.

I am more and more aware, as I age, that my life has been mostly successful, peaceful, happy and generative of goodness because of my parents' marriage, their perseverance, and their efforts to give me roots, an identity, and the possibility of a contributive and constructive vision for the continuance of life on this planet. My parents' sacramental marriage is bringing life to the coming generations of my family. Even after they have been forgotten as individuals, the grace of their lives is poured out into the lives of their progeny. Marriage is a sacrament that keeps on living long after two individuals verbalize commitment, unity, fidelity, and loving care for each other, and long after they die.

CHAPTER 20

Holy Orders

Priesthood, or as it is formally known, Holy Orders, is a sacrament of leadership, of spiritual pointing to the mystery of God, of demonstrating that there is a need in all people to be committed to service, justice, love, forgiveness, and rich and generous sharing, and for reminding all people that life is a sacrament, that life needs to be lived responsibly, deliberately, generously, and continuously for the sake of all people. Priesthood is about witness to the Gospel. Priesthood is about service to the needs of the individual, and to the health of society. Priesthood is a commitment to be a prophet, to remind oneself and those one serves that we are called to walk humbly with God and with each other.

Priesthood through the centuries has been a clarion call for all people who choose to listen, that the meaning, the invitation, the essence of the Gospel of Jesus Christ is to enhance life, to deepen respect for life, to ensure an ethic that will be disciplined enough to deliver dignity to and for life always- physical life, mental life, spiritual life, relational life, biological life, chemical life, ecological life, and a host of other dimensions of the energy of existence that we humans call "Life". We exist as part of a truth that is beyond comprehension, a truth called "Mystery". We share in the experience of creation, change, growth, emotional dynamics, intellectual searches, social involvements, and mystical moments.

We also, in our human journey, development and maturation, become aware at several different levels of being within ourselves, as we unfold new appreciation for the process of aging, of becoming more completely aware of what this journey is about, of realizing the importance of addressing possibility, potential, defeat, failure, betrayal, sin, and ultimately suffering and death. On our faith journey, the challenge to the priest, as I appreciate and understand it, is to walk with, to participate in, and to lead people to a deeper appreciation of the big truths of life that we call faith, hope and charity.

The Gospel of Jesus Christ has lasted for two thousand years, through periods of history that were confused, unethical, humanly and morally very wounded, and through social moments when next to nothing would seem to be of Christ. The spirit of truth, the "Holy Spirit", has worked through and with our imperfect humanity to advance all dimensions of truth, to inspire new efforts to develop God's creation, to empower our nature to continue to participate in the awareness of truth, the unfolding of creation, and to the correction and the redemption of our failures.

Priesthood is a profound experience and expression of pointing to the presence of God in all of life. It is a way of life that has been challenged throughout history, to point to the presence of God in Jesus Christ, and in His simple and constant teachings.

The fact that churches have filled up throughout all of history without great pressure from leadership speaks to the power of the human hunger for truth, for development, and for growth. The history of Christianity, as seen through the priesthood, is a movement toward truth, toward life, toward justice and charity. Our journey is an expression of the search for the Holy Grail, the Transcendent, the Eternal, and the Infinite. The human heart is a vision of the Spirit of God, an experience of sharing in God's Spirit, and an empowerment of that Spirit to share and continue this integrity of truth, life and love, for each other and for the future.

Visits to Prisons and Jails

My priesthood has been a tremendous blessing. I have experienced all that I have described in this book with the Christian people who have shared my journey and faith experience. This experience has opened doors of possibility for me to be involved in the lives of thousands of people, often on a one-time basis. I remember going to the Minnesota State Prison in Faribault, Minnesota. I offered Mass in that prison for those who wished to attend once a month, from 1991 to 1993. I have never seen those men again, and never will again in my life, but I was privileged to bring them to faith seeking truth beyond our comprehension, to hope of finding life beyond prison, and to charity for each other there in prison and beyond, to their families, their friends, and their co-workers.

The guard who usually took me from the front gate to the area of the prison in which Mass was celebrated, about two blocks away, was a young woman about twenty-five years of age. She probably weighed a hundred and fifteen pounds. As she and I walked along, we would meet several prisoners, Caucasian, African American, Mexican, Central American, and others. They would all greet my guard companion, saying, "Officer Judy, how are you?" And she would always respond, "Hi Joe, Hi Pete, Hi Cyril." She knew each of them by name. They respected her beyond words. She was not just a guard to them. She was that, but she was also a human being respecting another human being. I said to her one time, "Are you ever afraid of these people, being so small?" She said immediately, "No, I am not afraid. If ever any one of them would lay a hand on me, he would probably be killed by the other men." I told her that I so respected her because she respected them as human beings who had made mistakes, made imprudent choices, and acted irresponsibly. But she gave them the impression that they were redeemable, that they were good human beings who could, if they chose to do so, recover from painful, foolish and disruptive chapters in their lives.

Over the years I have visited in eight jails and prisons in Minnesota and Wisconsin. I have spoken to hundreds of men and dozens of women in the jails of these two states. I have shared with three murderers, several rapists, many bank robbers and armed robbers, many petty thieves, mostly drug addicts, drug dealers, drug sellers. I have shared with alcohol victims who broke the traffic laws. Some of them have sadly caused the death of one or more people, as they drove under the influence of alcohol.

Human tragedy is known, is painfully experienced, is adjudicated, and is described and pictured in the jails and prisons of America, as I have experienced them in the fifty years of my priesthood. What I have learned is that the vast majority of these people were wounded as human beings from their birth. They were born in poverty, almost always from families who had little or no education, from families broken by divorce, from families in which no real structure was present. Some did not know who their fathers were. Visits to jails inspire me to go back to the chalk board, to assess the basics of family life, the commitment of marriage, the stability of religious faith, human motivation, intellection, emotion, and perception.

The Life of Faith

This prison and jail ministry has probably helped me more than has any other experience to look deeply into the systems, the philosophy, the theology, the spirituality of our Church behavior, our Church presence, our Church teaching. Church structure can so easily distract me from the Gospel and the sacramental presence of Christ, which is what I have been ordained to offer to the people in my presence and charge.

Human Church law, Canon law, is so much a factor in the delivery of faith life that it sometimes, in my estimation, causes or enables us to abort the impact of the Gospel. Church law becomes *the* law, and sidelines the radical Gospel message and impact. Canon law is controlled by us humans because we promulgate the law, and so the law makes us feel secure managing the daily issues, problems and experiences of the Church structure of the moment.

The mystery of the Gospel, the movements of human experience, the complexity of birthing, living, and dying is a totally different, fluid picture that can only be negotiated as we come together in the "Sacrament of Community." We are in need of each other throughout life, but especially at dramatic, frightening, and challenging moments in our journey. The Gospel teaching is a web of truth as it reminds us again and again that we are one, one with God, one with each other, one with all of creation, one with all of spirit, one with time and eternity. Faith is truly a knowledge base that enables us to look beyond experience, to look beyond rationality, to look beyond human categories, limits, convictions and conventions.

We have a destiny beyond human knowledge, imagination, expectation and control. Most of us spend our lifetimes learning this simple but essential and inevitable truth. This is, I believe now, our faith journey, our faith walk, and our faith commitment. This has been my assignment, during fifty years of priesthood, in all of the assignments that I have had, in all the people with whom I have engaged life and experienced our common humanity. This is Christian life. This is the Catholic life that I have shared with so many others.

I am reminded frequently that my role is to look deeply into what makes us tick, what allows us to think through our many and various feelings, what allows us to decide life issues. I ask myself how I can inspire the young, sustain the committed people, and be present to the elderly, who are addressing a brand new dimension of our existence on this earth. In each era of our lives we learn, not so much by theory, but by walking the path of life attentively, intelligently, thoughtfully, reflectively.

The joy of priesthood is the Gospel of truth, of life, of love. What a privilege and what a challenge to deliver this gift to self and to others! Priesthood is as individual as those who are ordained to it, and as communal as the entire world. I have been privileged to offer Mass and the Sacraments to people from a humble rural church of thirteen families, located near Hart, which is outside of Rushford, Minnesota, to the largest parishes of our diocese, Queen of Angels Parish in Austin, the Cathedral of the Sacred Heart in Winona, St. Joseph Parish in Owatonna, and St. Augustine Parish in Austin.

The Anointing of the Sick

And finally, we Catholics recognize our mortality and the presence of suffering and death as part of our natural, essential, and uncontrolled journey in the Sacrament of Anointing of the Sick. It is not attractive for most of us, for most of our lives, to enter the classroom of suffering and death. In fact, we go there only because we are forced to do so by the circumstances of suffering and diminishment in our own lives and in the lives of our family and friends. But because this reality is part of every human life, our faith tradition has developed this Sacrament of Anointing of the Sick and dying, in order to assist all of us to deal with suffering and death, to define life in terms of mortality, and to call our attention to the mystery of life beyond the physical, beyond the obvious, and beyond the controllable dimensions of our existence on this earth.

CHAPTER 21

Personal Reminiscences and Reflections on the Sacraments

As a priest who has been active for almost fifty years, I have been involved in many sacraments and sacred moments with thousands of families. Using honest estimates, I feel certain that I have administered the Sacrament of Baptism, mostly to infants, at least 2,500 times. I have baptized approximately 250 adults. The day of the baptism of young peoples' children is a powerful moment in faith growth for the parents. Whatever their intention, whatever their reason for baptizing their child, somehow it seems that the parents are moved, changed, deepened in their appreciation of the mystery of life, in their perception of reality, destiny, meaning, and social involvement. They are experiencing, in the ritual of baptism, the deep responsibility that they have for the total development of their child. They appear to grasp the importance of a faith tradition, of a faith experience, a faith dimension, for the healthy and wholesome development of their child. They come to realize that their child is not only a member of their family. He or she is also a social being, involved in the lives of many other people, for the entirety of their existence on this earth. Religious identity, for most people, is a profound and important aspect of that realization and appreciation, as the child grows into experiencing society.

We all know that as we grow up we are identified as a family member by our name and by our blood. We also have a social need to belong to the greater community, socially, culturally, and for most of us, religiously. C. S. Lewis, the famed English author, wrote of many mysteries. In one of his writings, over one hundred and twenty years ago, he observed, "We are a soul; we have a body." That truth seems to be buried deeply in the spiritual, intellectual, emotional, and social dimensions of our lives as Catholic Christians. Healthy and happy life is not only individual. It is also social, an essential part of our nature. We continue to find our identities, our meaning, our importance in and to creation as we live into and through social experiences and relationships.

I have been privileged to confirm in our Catholic tradition of faith more than 250 adults, and have helped to prepare approximately 2,500 adolescent people for Confirmation. In the Catholic tradition, the bishop is the normal minister of Confirmation, except for emergency situations, when a priest is permitted to administer the sacrament. Most young people today do not practice their Catholic faith very frequently, by going to Mass regularly or by celebrating the Sacrament of Reconciliation on a regular basis. But they do want to belong to the tradition of faith in which they have been raised. They believe in the mystery of God. They believe in the teachings of Jesus, as recorded in the New Testament. But they do not feel that they need to attend church every week. They want the Church and its ministry to be present, and they want to engage it at meaningful moments in their lives.

I have worked with and witnessed the marriages of at least 1,500 couples over the last fifty years. I have validated a few hundred marriages of people who were first married outside the Catholic Church.

Another very significant observance is the celebrating of wedding anniversaries with extended families. Popular milestones for these celebrations are at twenty-five years, forty years, fifty years, and sixty or more years. They are almost always happy, peaceful and enriching for all who participate. Wedding anniversaries are part of the glue that helps younger families persevere through the rough times of intimacy, family life, and marital stress.

I have for years encouraged couples who were approaching forty or more years of marriage to hold a celebration, if for no other reason, for their children and grandchildren. Their families have known the stresses, hard times, vulnerable times in the marriage. It is a powerful experience for the young to watch their parents, who have survived the stresses of marriage, renew their own determination to live the intimacy of marriage through perseverance, mutual forgiveness, and determination to provide stability to their respective families and children.

The most memorable experience I have of a marriage vow renewal celebration happened more than forty years ago. I have told this story to young couples many times, as I work with them to prepare for their own marriage. I believe this story represents the essence of love, perseverance, mutual respect and disciplined charity in life.

I was serving as Principal of Cotter High School in Winona, Minnesota at the time. One day in May a senior girl came to the office and asked if she could speak with me. I invited her into the office. She was quite nervous, so I tried to calm her, and asked what I could do for her. She asked, "Would you ever be willing to come to my great-grandparents' home to have a renewal of their marriage vows?" I said that I would be honored to do that for her. She immediately lightened up, was very happy and enthusiastic, and said something like, "May I get back to you on possible dates for this to happen?" I told her to do just that, and before the day was over I received a phone call from her mother, and the date for the renewal was set. It was on a Sunday afternoon in early June of 1969 or 1970.

I went to the humble, small house of the great-grandparents on the appointed day, on the east side of Winona. There were approximately two-hundred relatives and friends in the small house, on the roof of that house, on the roofs of the neighbors' houses, and in the yard. I entered the house and was taken to the bedroom, where the great-grandparents were at that moment. Grandpa was in bed in a frail condition, and Grandma was sitting on the side of the bed, near her husband. I greeted them, and then asked for silence, as we would renew the marriage vows. Both of them were ninety-nine years of age, and they were celebrating their eightieth wedding anniversary. That was the oldest wedding anniversary I have ever celebrated.

After the renewal of their vows, I asked if they remembered anything from their wedding day that they could share with their family. Grandpa could not remember anything, but Grandma said, "Yes, I remember that, at the end of the wedding, as the priest was dismissing us, before we left the altar he leaned down and whispered to us, 'Now, you two be good to each other.'" At that point she placed her hand on the hand of her husband, and after eighty years of marriage she said, "We have been good to each other." This is the most beautiful love story I have ever heard in fifty years of priesthood. It happened in a simple, moderately poor home on the east side of Winona, Minnesota.

I am certain that moment has blessed the generations of that particular family, and of their friends, for the last forty-five years. Lived witness speaks a thousand times louder than any words of parents, preachers, teachers, or professors. To live the truth, to live charity, forgiveness and love, to live in faith and hope- these are the movements, the energies, the spirits which move human beings to growth, to peace, to justice, to respect for each other, and to a willingness to continue the human spirit of communion, reverence for all of creation, and to a sacrificial spirit of working tirelessly to bring people together, to dialogue out differences of opinion on any and all issues, and to find common ground that can save, rather than destroy, individuals, families and communities.

I have assisted several hundred Catholic divorced people who have wanted to pursue what is known as an annulment, which is a canon (Church) law look at the health and the validity of their broken marriage from the very beginning. The annulment process is a very difficult and controversial practice, even among Catholics. But some people are comforted by going through this very long (usually a year), thorough, and painful process of looking at their failed marriage. This annulment process does help some Catholics. Others, both Catholic and non-Catholic, want nothing to do with the experience.

On Death and Dying

I have officiated at more than 2,000 funerals in fifty years. It is a privilege, almost beyond words, to share with families in this difficult and emotionally charged time. Families remember what happened at their loved one's funeral perhaps better than any other event or dimension of the deceased person's life. If the funeral is conducted properly, kindly, attentively, and with sensitivity, the family is usually, in my experience, comforted, healed and strengthened to move on with life, while grieving the irreversible change that happens at the death of a loved one.

After a death, one of the most important experiences for the family is to have a positive time as they plan the funeral for their loved one. They are saying goodbye. They are adjusting to an irreversible change in their lives, as they must go on without the loved one, as they prepare to speak about this unique experience with their friends, neighbors, co-workers. There is no textbook written for this movement. We learn the path by walking it, and by sharing the emotions, thoughts, doubts, worries, fears and insecurities, with family or friends or counselors as one chooses, so that we can resolve the pain of the present and find a way to life after death.

The death experience seems to be a moment of growth, shifting perceptions, and challenging ideas for many of us. A family is forever changed when a member of the family dies. Death usually drags us into our most unvisited emotions, our deepest insecurities, our strongest fears. We only go there because we are forced to go there. Death demands that we see things differently and that we look at each other, and the world, differently. Death turns a corner in our lives that enables us to look back, but never to go back. Life is ongoing in all of its aspects, one of which is the experience that we call death, and there is no changing of the circumstances in which we find ourselves. Our choices are involved with how we will interpret the current reality and how we will respond to that reality.

If the funeral is not conducted in a reverent, comforting, respectful fashion, the family, to some degree, never gets over the moment. I have heard of a few of these cases in which the cleric has been insensitive, angry, or inappropriate. Hearing these sad stories has been a continuing reminder to me to be attentive, to be present, to listen carefully, and to respect the family's needs at the time of death, and during the planning of the funeral. These moments are very crucial for all involved.

Survivors of death differ in their emotional, spiritual and religious conditions. One size, one approach, does not fit all families or individual members of families in these emotionally charged moments. Family history, the individual's life experiences, personal impressions of the meaning of death and the afterlife- all of these things and more are intensely at play as one walks the path of loss, grief, radical change, emotional instability, and irreversible reality.

Death reveals and amplifies family unity or family anger, brokenness, and divisions. Joy and pain are frequent reactions of families as they prepare for, and live through, the funeral experience. Family emotional history, social history, relational history, are all uncovered at the time of a death. It seems to uncover emotions, memories, divisions, and other negative experiences that have perhaps been buried for years.

This is a moment, an opportunity, a possibility for an outsider, the priest, to assist the family in possibly healing some of that pain. In my experience, sometimes I have been able to help, but unfortunately, in some cases the family has been so broken, for so long, that any attempt to bring them together has radically and sadly failed.

Conversely, most families, at the time of death of one of their members, come together in support of each other, in comforting each other, in planning for the most fitting and appropriate funeral for their loved one. It is always a joy to sit with families as we plan the funeral and hear them tell the life-giving stories about the deceased. The family members laugh and cry, appreciate what the deceased family member had given them, how he or she had ticked them off- all of the good things that had happened between and with them.

One of the most sacred and treasured experiences for me, as a priest, is to be able to sit at the bedside of a dying person, to invite her or him to speak of the emotions, perceptions, the questions, the doubts and fears, the wonderment of the dying process. It is a sacred and sobering moment for the patient with whom I am speaking and listening, and for me.

I have learned over the years of helping people prepare for their death, of the importance of listening actively. By that description of listening, I mean that by listening very attentively and carefully the dying person gives me the lead-in for the next question, observation, or verbal reaction on my part. I continue to learn every day that listening in life is one of the greatest gifts we can give to each other, and listening at the time of death is the ultimate gift.

First Reconciliation

I have been involved with approximately 2,500 children as they prepared for their first Holy Communion, and have heard the first confessions of at least that many young children. I have many wonderful stories about first confessions.

The first story is my own. About twenty years ago I celebrated an anniversary Mass for a Franciscan Sister at Assisi Heights in Rochester, Minnesota. I mentioned in the homily that it was a Franciscan Sister who heard my first confession! This was at St. Bridget's Church near Simpson, Minnesota, located ten miles south of Rochester. Of course, it was not really an official Confession. The Sister who was teaching us second grade students about first Confession took us into the confessional and acted as the priest, and we kids confessed our terrible seven-year-old crimes to her. This story of mine offended some people.

Another first Confession story happened at the Cathedral Church in Winona more than forty years ago. I was hearing the confessions of these little people, and as I was listening to a little boy through the screen of the confessional on my left, I could hear the sobs of the child in the confessional compartment on my right. She was so distressed that I said to the little boy who was confessing to me, "Please let me close this window for a moment. I will be right back." He said, "OK," so I closed his screen and opened the one on the other side of the confessional to the wailing of the poor child who was there, obviously frightened to death. I said to her, "Are you OK?" She wailed, "No!" I said, "What is wrong?" She said, "I need to go to the bathroom." I said, "Well, just open your door and go out, and a teacher will help you." She said, "No, I have already gone to the bathroom," and indeed she had. I whisked her off through the side door and a teacher mercifully came and helped the poor child clean up.

Another wonderful story about first Confession involved a little boy seven years old. He came into the confessional, came around the screen and sat before me to make his confession. He admitted that he had disobeyed his parents, he had told a few lies, he had fought with his sister, he had not shared his toys with his sister. Then he paused for a moment and studied me intently. He said, "And I have one more really big sin." I said to him something like, "Well, you just wait, and when you are ready, just tell God what your really big sin is." Again he paused for a few seconds, and then blurted out, "I called my cat 'a son-of-a-bitch'." It was clear to me in that moment that what the little guy did not tell me was that his mother had heard him and told him to tell the priest about "this really big one." ‡

‡ EDITOR'S NOTE: Additional discussion of the sacraments may be found in Chapter 24 of the following section, and throughout this book.

SECTION V

THE SPIRITUAL LIFE AND FURTHER REFLECTIONS ON THE SACRAMENTS

CHAPTER 22

Spirituality

Each of us lives our existence made up of physical, biological, chemical, intellectual and spiritual dimensions. Each aspect of our being contributes essentially to human existence. The spiritual piece of our life is somehow involved with our personality, with our history, and with our family. Our spirituality determines, I think, our potential for happiness, fulfillment, and healthy development throughout life. Without a healthy spirit, physiology, biology, chemistry and intellectual energy do not add up to a peaceful life.

I can remember my spirit developing from the time I was five years old. I remember that I lived with my family in a farm house that did not have electricity or running water. Those two realities defined life for me as a young child. I vividly remember when the day of miracles came as an electric light appeared in our yard for the first time on a tall pole. This, I learned, as the days went by, was the yard light. From that source of energy we could pump water and throw away our lanterns, which previously were the only source of light in our house, barn, and everywhere else we went in the dark.

Eventually, we were able to dismiss the outhouse and get an indoor bathroom (What a gift!!!), an electric furnace, and other simple appliances which revolutionized life for us. As farmers, when we could afford a milking machine it brought great joy, less hard labor, and a saving of time that we had never known. My spirituality is tied to all of these very real and foundational memories.

Spirit is the experience and the realization that determines the development of life for each of us. Spirit is the undefinable, but real aspect of human life that determines how our lives unfold. A big piece of my spirit, and of our family's spirit, was our Catholic faith in Jesus Christ. My earliest memories involved church, prayer at night and in the morning, seeing my parents sometimes kneeling at their bedside before they went to bed. I also learned early on what it meant to be a discipline of charity, sharing with and forgiving my brothers, as they came along. I learned that I had to be responsible for simple chores in the house and around the farm. As I reflect, all of this was foundational to my spiritual development.

As I have aged, I have come to know more and more that spirituality does not have to be primarily religious. My spirituality is the essence of who I am, of who I am coming to be on each new day. My spirituality certainly involves my religious faith and convictions, but my spirituality also involves my thoughts, my feelings, my joys and sorrows, my successes and my failures, all of my relationships with human beings, with my dog Salley, and with all of God's creation.

My spirituality is tied to my willingness to mature, to change, to grow. Spirituality is dynamic, never finished, never stopped. It is not restricted to one period of life. The ancient philosophers experienced the reality of spirituality and taught that reality to their children: "The only constant in life is change!". Our spirit is defined by each breath we take, by each experience we have, and by each moment that passes. Our spirituality, as I understand it, teaches us constantly that to live is to be, and to live is to continuously become and develop into a new, wiser, richer, more peace-filled person. Spirituality is communion with the mystery of God, with all of creation, with all of experience, and with awareness of the present moment.

To be present to life is the secret of a rich spirituality. A Christian discipline in the spirit must continuously bring the mind home. We quiet our spirit as we get reacquainted with our life, with our soul, with our deepest being, at each new moment of conscious life.

Spirituality is, in my experience, the basis of inspiration, creativity, perseverance and courage. It seems to me that without a healthy spirit I cannot garner enough strength to generously contribute to life, to enrich life and to demonstrate life to the next generation in a manner that opens their hearts to new and unexplored possibilities for the advancement of their own lives.

Enthusiasm is one of my favorite pursuits. Etymologically, the word "enthusiasm" comes from the Greek and it means to be in God and to have God in us. Enthusiasm for life has been for me a constant and clarion call to deepen spirit, to enrich spirit, to enhance spirit in life.

Spirituality is the all-encompassing dimension of human life that continuously leads us to depth, to enrichment, to more profound appreciation of the gift that life is and can become every day. Spirituality is for me the energy that slows my pace to see the world around me that sustains me, and to find new avenues of the world within me that enhance and challenge me to move on, to engage life, and to know the potential that invites me to growth.

Spirituality is the Holy Spirit of God that lives within each of us. As Christians, we are taught, and I deeply believe, that we are all made in the image of God, that somehow we participate in the Spirit of God, and that our journey is a round trip to and from the source of all life: God Almighty. What a journey! What a story! What an exciting experience!

CHAPTER 23

The Seminary Experience

A very central, essential and empowering aspect of my life as a priest was, and is, the prayerful, contemplative, inspirational, and deepening spiritual journey of life. In the seminary, from 1953 through 1961, spirituality was always liturgical, meaning that we prayed together, we meditated in the same space as all of our brothers; we did what we were told to do. As a beginning chapter for a life of spiritual deepening, that was a good experience. It was a painful discipline that leads to direction, strength, and a persevering attitude. I am grateful for this start, challenging as it was!

When I was ordained a priest, a huge emphasis on spiritual development and the sustained energy of a healthy spiritual life included the *Divine Office*, a Latin prayer read for about fifty minutes a day. It included the Psalms, readings from the ancient spiritual fathers (and mothers), and reflections on the spiritual journey throughout history. We were also encouraged to pray the rosary every day. The rosary is a reflective prayer of meditation on the mysteries of Christ's life and of our own life. It was a monotonous, repetitive and demanding attraction to meditate on the idea of the moment. It was, and is, a mental and spiritual instrument of discipline, direction, focus and reflection that opens our souls to deepening appreciation and involvement in the mystery of God present through Jesus, Mary, and all of humanity.

We also traditionally meditated before we celebrated Mass each morning. Silent, focused, disciplined mental control was part of the search for the mystery of God, and a strong avenue of our spiritual journey into human and spiritual growth, as well as our growth in social awareness. I am grateful for that discipline, that direction, and that emphasis on the need to discipline our minds, our spirits, and our bodies. Such discipline was needed if we hoped to be effective leaders in this demanding and life-giving journey of faith, opened to truth bigger than we can comprehend; to hope, which is larger than the life we know; and to charity, which challenges us to the limits, as we address intimate care, respect, and love for each other.

Physical, mental and spiritual life need management and ownership on the part of the Christian if he or she hopes to develop, to deepen appreciation of the mystery, and continue to grow. Our Christian spiritual practices are historically proven behaviors that help develop the courageous perseverance necessary for attaining a real and deep spiritual life.

In my experience, the spiritual life of Jesus Christ must be studied, worked at, and earned. It is then that we are involved in the mystery of Christ to the degree needed to deepen our souls, to bring peace to our hearts, to enable us to grow into a willingness to pass this spirit on to those who follow us.

Another aspect of the spiritual training and practice that we all observed throughout our eight years of Seminary training was the so-called "Grand Silence." This practice began each evening when we prayed *Compline*, the official night office prayer of the pre-Vatican II Church. It was approximately ten minutes of recited Psalms, scripture, prayer and song (usually Gregorian chant) which was sung a cappella. Night prayer was prayed at 9:30 PM. Lights were to be out by 10:00 PM, partly because we all would be roused by a bell at 5:30 AM. We had to be in our places in chapel by 6:00 AM for meditation, which was usually led by a priest, who served as the Spiritual Director of our program. We always wore the cassock, which is a long flowing black robe. We lived in the garment, except for the one hour per day when we recreated and exercised.

After night prayer there was never talking to each other until after meditation, Mass and breakfast in the morning. The only exception to this Grand Silence rule and practice would be an emergency. This practice was a discipline to deepen our spirit, to set the stage for prayer and reflection, and practically, to keep the halls of the dormitories silent and quiet to ensure rest for all occupants, usually about thirty seminarians on a floor, each in a small private room. Each room had a bed, straight-back chair, a desk, a small closet, and a sink.

We also ate our meals in silence most of the time. We always had a brief reading by one of the seminarians at the beginning of our meals. These readings were usually brief excerpts from early Christian writers. In the major seminary, the deacons, who were in their last year of training, always gave a homily as we ate lunch. In those days we had typewriters, and would be required to have enough copies of the homily made so that each faculty member would have the copy before him at the head table as the deacon spoke. This copying was a laborious and painful practice which ate up tons of carbon paper, and long periods of time, as we erased each typing error on all of the carbon copies.

Seminary education and formation in the pre-Vatican II Church, prior to 1964, for me involved four years of college at St. Mary's College in Winona, Minnesota, earning a degree with a Philosophy major and Latin and Education minors. We studied four years of Latin in college, and two years of Greek, and as many of the liberal arts courses as we could fit into our time possibilities. Included in these courses were General Psychology, Educational Psychology, and Abnormal Psychology. We had to pass a Latin and Greek examination when we graduated from college, because all of our textbooks in the major seminary, the final four years of training, were written in Latin. Fifty years later, I am still somewhat fluent in Latin, having been exposed to it so much in my training.

Our academic program in the major seminary involved four years of scripture study, five days a week; four years of Church History study, five days a week; two years of Dogmatic Theology, two years of Moral Theology, and two years of Sacramental Theology. Also included were courses in Homiletics, Liturgy, Catechesis, and Spirituality.

Every student on entering the major seminary was tested for his musical ability. If he passed the audition he was automatically assigned to the choir. I was assigned to the choir, which in my day consisted of about 120 voices. Our music director was a task master, but we did learn music. We were an excellent choir. Our proudest musical presentation was *Palestrina* in four voice parts, sung a cappella.

Each day in the seminary we were forced to go outside for exercise and recreation for one hour a day. If the weather was too severe, we went to the gym. We were not allowed to leave the campus without explicit permission; and if we received permission, we rode public transportation, never in a private automobile. We were not allowed to have a car at the seminary. A few of my fellow students snuck a car into the neighborhood of the seminary, but they and their car were soon no longer part of the seminary! The discipline of the fifties in seminaries was clearly defined, constantly enforced, and held dire consequences for the offender. The breaking of a single rule resulted in immediate expulsion. Every one of us knew that this was the practice. I am certain now, as I look back, that it was that spirit which enabled the staff at the seminary to control approximately 300 young men effectively, efficiently, and with immediacy.

In the 1950's there were seminaries spread throughout the country for high school boys. Once they had graduated eighth grade, at thirteen or fourteen years of age, boys were invited into the seminary. One such seminary was Nazareth Hall, located in St. Paul, Minnesota and operated by the Archdiocese of Saint Paul.

When I went to Saint Paul Seminary, located adjacent to St. Thomas University, on the banks of the Mississippi river in Saint Paul, several of my class-mates were graduates of Nazareth Hall high school seminary. These guys were bright people, wonderful academics, good friends, and people who brought laughter and humor to almost any moment when a group of us would be together. At this point in our training, we were all college graduates, twenty-one or twenty-two years of age, and open to getting on with a challenging curriculum and the discipline of the major seminary. That is exactly what we did.

CHAPTER 24

Ordination and Beyond

In 1961, fifty of us men from Saint Paul Seminary were ordained to priesthood for several dioceses, located in Illinois, Wisconsin, Minnesota, Nebraska, and North and South Dakota. We spread out to our various assignments in ministry, teaching, and hospital work throughout that six state region.

Within the first year of our ordination, one of my classmates, and one of my best friends, Fr. Pat Roache, died of throat cancer at the Methodist Hospital in Rochester, Minnesota. With Pat's death, forty-nine of us priests remained from our class, to serve God's people in six states in the upper Midwest area of the United States.

Fast-forward to our fifteenth anniversary of ordination, the year 1976. Now, most of us were forty-one or forty-two years of age. As we arrived at our fifteenth class reunion, held at a resort on the St. Croix River, just east of St. Paul, Minnesota, we began to greet classmates, some of whom we had not seen for fifteen years. Physical changes, especially weight and graying hair, were the openings for humor, getting re-acquainted, and happily greeting each other.

That first evening of our three-day gathering featured a wonderful social hour, meal, and sharing of the last fifteen years for each of us. In the course of the evening, I grew up quite a bit. As each man told his story, our class was redefined radically. We all still were, for the most part, happy men, but directions in our lives had changed significantly. Of the forty-nine of us still living, twenty-five men had chosen, over the fifteen years since we were ordained, to leave the Catholic priestly ministry. Most of these men had chosen marriage, and were now beginning their families. As near as I could tell, they were happy with their decisions. As we concluded that reunion, a class of fifty priests had been reduced by one death and twenty-five men choosing to leave priestly ministry for another way of life. That meant that, after fifteen years since ordination for fifty men, fifty-two percent chose another approach to the mystery of God, life, and experience for their journey.

The vast majority of the men who chose to leave the priesthood were people who had been in the high school seminary. Two of these men are still my close friends, and they have intimated several times that, as adolescent boys, they had never experienced falling in love, becoming infatuated with a girl, or learning to negotiate the emotional and sexual challenges of this time of life. They had been tucked away in the safety of the high school seminary, where sexual, emotional, social and psychological realities were suppressed, negated, and ignored.

I am saddened for our Catholic tradition of faith in the Lord that there are currently movements alive to bring back high school seminaries. These movements are almost always instigated by the clergy, who are apparently seeking to control the clerical cast, formation and development of men who are considering priesthood. In modern history, it is overwhelmingly demonstrated that boys should grow up at home with parents, siblings, and natural social contacts in order to have the healthiest, most balanced psyche, and the best appreciation of society, sexuality, personal responsibility, and social interaction with others. My own prejudiced view is that the home is the best seminary preparation place and setting for men who consider a celibate way of life in the ministry. Mother and Father are much wiser than any professor, academe or counselor who perhaps occasionally touches a young person's life.

Since the eleventh century, when celibacy became the rule for clergy, the hierarchy and the clergy have become more closed, more demanding as to the way the system is to work, as to the meaning of spiritual leadership, and as to the governance imposed on the laity. People are walking away from our tradition in the hundreds of thousands significantly because of this attitude, this stance, this rule governing the Catholic structure, exclusively, from the top down. Our Catholic tradition of faith is, in my estimation, on a downward spiral, which means that people are leaving our church tradition. The influence of our ethical positions and of our philosophy of life is being sidelined or ignored, and our social influence as a group of sincere Christian people is being diminished constantly.

This history of fifty years of clerical experience is, for me, a significant invitation to the hierarchy and clerical leadership of our Catholic tradition of faith in the Lord Jesus to look again at the clerical underpinnings of our faith tradition. The last fifty years have issued a clarion call, in my mind, for the entire Church membership, clerical and lay, to look at Church law, leadership, psychology, spirituality, sociology and style, as we point to the future as a viable tradition, to support our ancient and rich sacramental and biblical offerings for the spiritual growth of the people. Our world has changed, is changing every second, and will continue to experience acceleration in the phenomenon of change. Our challenge as Catholics, in my mind, is to keep the stability of the Gospel values alive in the continuously changing applications of life dynamically happening all of the time.

Human perception, appreciation and involvement in the speed of technological change in our present life situation must be kept healthy, alert, aware, and opened to new needs, new awareness, new calls, new opportunities, as we travel together through this experience that we call life. Meaning is at least as important as experience. Our spiritual foundation is the launch pad for continued participation in the creative and redemptive process of our world.

CHAPTER 25

The Sacraments and the Community

The Roman Catholic gift to Christianity, in my view, is the effort to live and offer and promote the seven Sacraments, which highlight and focus attention on all of the developmental aspects of life as well as on the diminishment of life, as each of us experiences body and mind breakdown, leading eventually to death. The Sacraments are the call to the community to be involved in the life of each individual all along the way. This is the sacredness of faith, hope and charity.

For centuries history has celebrated these aspects of life within the Catholic tradition. Sacraments are social and individual experiences. Sacraments highlight for all who choose to be part of them, the various times, developmental periods in each life, and Sacraments always lead us more deeply into the mystery of God. Sacraments have been very rich experiences for me throughout all of the years of my life,

and of my priesthood. Sacraments are intimate con-
nections between people that mark the various important moments and experiences of our life journey.

Baptism

We baptize most of our Roman Catholic members as infants or children, and the Sacrament of Baptism welcomes them into our homes and community.
The celebration of the Sacrament is a welcoming and
sanctifying gesture, but is also a teaching moment for
the parents, for the entire family, and for the greater
community. Baptism reminds us frequently in life that
we do belong to the Body of Christ. We are one with
Christ and with each other. The Gospel teaches us that
Christian responsibility toward each other, with each
other, and in support of each other, is constant, essential to our Christian way of living, and is the witness
to others that we believe in love, forgiveness, justice
and peace.

The Sacrament of Reconciliation

As our children grow, we introduce them to the
Sacrament of Reconciliation. The movement and gift

in this sacred moment and experience for the children, who usually celebrate this Sacrament at about age seven or eight, is a teaching to them that they must work at being responsible for their young lives. The Sacrament of Reconciliation is pointed at healthy mental, spiritual, social, and mystical development for each of the young people who prepare for this sacrament and then experience the sacrament. This sacrament is an individual experience, but it is also a social teaching and reminder that culture cannot survive unless each of us practices the spirit of truth, integrity, charity and justice, to name but a few of the dimensions of the teachings of Jesus Christ.

Mental health is tied to emotional stability, social integrity, and a religious life that is constant in its efforts to renew and be redeemed, to be willing to take new directions as we experience new areas of life, new challenges. The Sacrament of Reconciliation addresses these aspects of our being, mental health, spiritual awareness, social openness, and cultural involvement. All of us hopefully develop a strength that contributes to this reality for the sake of our culture. Reconciliation empowers a person to own his or her soul. Physical, mental and emotional integrity cannot be operative if the spirit is not at peace.

Reconciliation is the experience, the opportunity to bring our soul home, to make peace with our mistakes, to rejoice in our growth, and to make sincere efforts at redirecting our life. This is a sacred, a sacramental experience of life.

As a discipline in my life since I was ordained a priest, I have tried to go to confession once a month. This sacrament has been for me a challenge, a comfort, a continuing call and reminder to have integrity, to live priesthood to the best of my ability, and to face my weaknesses, my sinfulness, and my struggles. Reconciliation has been a wonderful gift for me personally throughout my life. Perhaps I am a priest today because of this sacrament.

I have heard confessions at least every other day of the fifty years of my priesthood. I sat down some time ago and tried to estimate the number of times that I have been privileged to offer absolution to a sorrowful, confessing penitent. I know that I must have heard twenty-five to thirty thousand confessions over the years. Most of these I have heard in the church, but I have also heard them in jails and prisons. I have celebrated this sacrament with others in hospitals, in rest homes, and in private homes.

As I try to estimate numbers in my priesthood, I know that I have experienced more than 6,000 hospital visits and more than 6,000 rest home visits, as well as at least 6,000 private home visits. I have heard confessions on many of these visits. I have heard confessions as the penitent and I walked through the woods, and as we casually strolled down the street. I have heard them in cars and in trucks, on trains, on ships, and a few times as we flew across the world in jets.

The confession of a dying person is a very humbling and intense event. A great gift of our faith practice is to make available to dying people the opportunity to confess their failings, their selfishness, and their sinfulness. In my experience, the dying find great peace in this sacrament. People who have been away from this sacrament for thirty, forty, fifty or more years come and want to find their way to peace of mind, to the deeper mystery of truth, to peace with their families, with themselves.

I have heard the confession of a murderer twice, of rapists a few times, of armed robbers, and of people who have been involved in hate crimes several times. I have heard the confessions of several female prostitutes, and of a few male prostitutes. I have heard the confessions of mentally and emotionally ill people who have desperately been looking for more peace.

A great gift to the priesthood is the ability to hear confessions. But it is hard work, too- at least for me. As confessor, I try my best to pay close attention to what the penitent says, because this message is life-changing, life-giving, and life-saving. The mind, the emotions, the truth of life, which includes the failures of the penitent, are being exposed. Usually the penitent is nervous because she or he is exposing their innermost being.

On a retreat almost forty years ago, the director of the retreat was talking to us priests as confessors. I have always remembered the analogy he gave about the penitent, as he or she goes to confession. The director said something like, "When we go to the doctor and have to undress, most of us are a bit self-conscious. When someone comes to you as a confessor, they are undressing their soul as they confess their vulnerability, their weakness, and their failures to you; and that is usually more traumatic than undressing our body." I remember that to this day because, at least in most cases of people coming to confession, that saying is the truth.

I have told lay people many times in my life that I wish that every Catholic could hear confessions for a couple of hours in their adult life. Their lives would be changed for the better as they heard the confessions.

I have heard confessions in about ten jails and prisons through the years, in Minnesota and Wisconsin. I estimate that I have visited at least five hundred people in jails and prisons, the vast majority of whom have been men. From this experience, I can only conclude that women are smarter than men!

My favorite story about the Sacrament of Reconciliation (confession) involves a young man in one of the jails in which I offered Mass for those inmates who chose to participate. After Mass, I told them that I would be in the next room to hear confessions for any of them who wished to confess. The wall between the two rooms was an inch of glass, and so as I sat in the confessional space waiting for the penitents to come, one at a time, I could see the others on the other side of the glass wall. On this particular evening four men were waiting to confess. As they approached the confessional space, I became more and more aware that the last young man in the confessional line was very nervous. He was moving from side to side and wringing his hands.

When his turn finally came, he entered the room, shook my hand, and with a heavy sigh sat down to confess. He then said something like, "Man, I hope that I will do this right. I have been talking with my buddies about this." I said to him something like, "Just take your time, and when you are ready to tell the Lord what you want to say, just relax and say it."

This young man knew the formula for the sacrament, and had obviously examined his conscience thoroughly. He made an excellent confession of his sins and failings. When he finished, he said, "I sure hope that I did that right because this is my first time;

and besides that, I am Lutheran!" I assured him that
he had done a better job at the sacrament than do
many Catholics.

The Sacrament of the Eucharist

The Sacrament of Eucharist is as ancient as the
Sacrament of Baptism. Baptism celebrates our social
responsibility and involvement, and Eucharist continues to feed us, reminding us of our absolute depend-
ence on God, of our union with Jesus Christ, as mystical people on a journey. Our children are introduced
to this experience at age seven or eight. First Communion, in our tradition, is a sacred moment, when a
person, usually a child, comes face to face with the
mystery of God, experienced in a symbol, a sacrament. First Communion furthers a child's ability to
see what is not physically present, to appreciate what
cannot be controlled or contained or radically owned.
First Communion introduces us to the depth of mystery, to the presence of God in all times, in all things,
in all experiences.

Life does not make sense totally without the
transcendent. First Holy Communion brings us to that
transcendental moment and experience and realization
that we live in mystery. Holy Communion is about

humanity, person, the mystery of God, the courage to enter mystery, the willingness to grow in every dimension of our nature and being as humans.

Holy Communion invites us to approach the mystery of God and the reality of love and forgiveness with and for each other. Holy Communion enjoins us again and again to be social, to be with and for each other to the very best of our ability. Holy Communion is the sacrament that helps us to grow optimally as human beings, as social beings, as beings willing to open ourselves continuously, throughout life, to the mystery of God present. Holy Communion keeps us centered on humanity, on integrity, on eternity.

Children do not know the full meaning of the Eucharist. Neither do their parents and neither do the priests, who are ordained to confect Eucharist in the name of the people, and in the name of Jesus Christ. We all together participate in this experience, this mystery, this movement, this sacrament, which continually inspires our lives and renews our willingness and courage to go on. The Eucharist is the greatest gift that parents and Church offer a child at age seven. The child does not know that fact, and neither do the people who offer the Eucharistic gift. Participating in, not controlling the mystery of Eucharist is the attraction and the power of the sacrament. We are called and experienced beyond ourselves in Eucharist. It is the sacrament that insists that we let go of control in life and that we responsibly manage control of that part of life which is in our observance, but Eucharist also teaches us again and again to be humble creatures before our God.

The Eucharist is the central truth, mystery, experience of the Christian world. This fact has to be the reason that I enjoy so much celebrating Mass with people in times of joy, in times of tragedy and sorrow, in times of fear and insecurity, in any circumstance that life can hand us. The Communion of Jesus Christ with his people, who comprise the Church, is the union of the world as it affects Christian people, and is the energy that drives a significant part of the world.

Confirmation

For the past several years, Confirmation has been celebrated in our diocese at the sophomore level of high school. I believe this is an appropriate age to ask these emerging young adults to make a commitment to their faith, to their family, and to themselves. Confirmation is the moment when we begin to look out of ourselves, out of our tendency to magic, out of self-centered childhood. Confirmation is about maturing as a person, as a Christian, and as a social being who must find meaning for life in the social aspect of our existence. We are not rugged individuals, as our American cowboy/cowgirl philosophy tends to dictate. We are social beings, essentially involved with and for each other.

Confirmation invites us into a deeper examination of life, of meaning, of involvement with the people who touch our lifes. As I have worked with young people over all the years, as they prepare for celebrating the Sacrament of Confirmation, I have found those who say that they are being confirmed in our Catholic tradition of faith only because their parents or their grandparents want them to be so. Other young people are searching for the richer experience of faith that leads to a bigger truth, hope that inspires us to more life, and charity that is the only lasting glue for society.

Adolescence is a period of life, I have found, that exhibits many emotions, passions, perceptions, and convictions about life that are constantly on the move and that are constantly changing. This is the reason that I never come down hard on an adolescent who seems belligerent, reactive, full of doubts and questions, and tends to reject all that his or her parents have offered as a way of life. This is the searching process. This is adolescent spirituality. This is the way, the truth and the life of many, if not most adolescent people in our culture, as I have experienced them.

The experience of the Sacrament of Confirmation for young people is a significant moment for the individual being confirmed, for parents and families, and for the greater community. This is because it reminds all of us, at every age, that we are pilgrims, that we are searchers, and that we seek God however, whomever, whatever that is. Confirmation is, as are all the sacraments, an instrument of faith that touches individuals and all the members of the community.

I served as a high school principal in three different schools, Winona Cotter for ten years, Mankato Loyola for one year, and Austin Pacelli for three years. In all of these communities I found good young people who were searching for life, for life's meaning, for methods of making valid individual choices, for independent thinking. I learned from the young again and again that we find our way via questions, never via answers. Confirmation is the sacrament of questions and of questioning. This sacrament is about the unsettled moments of life search, of life turmoil, and of life contradictions.

This Sacrament of Confirmation is not only a clear call to those being confirmed in their faith. This sacrament is also a renewed invitation to all Catholic Christians to learn to walk in faith, with questions, with doubts, with unfinished business in terms of the mystery of God. Confirmation is a consecration of growth, development and maturation, for all involved in the mystery of the Christ walk. Humility is a fruit of this sacrament because it holds out for us, one more time, the need to be creature before our Creator.

SECTION VI

THE CHURCH IN THE MODERN WORLD

CHAPTER 26

The Church in the Modern World

To this point in these memoirs I have focused on my beginnings, education, and development in life, my arrival at ordination and the chronology of professional assignments, some of the stories of the experiences that accompanied my assignments and musings on the meaning of all this. Theological and Sacramental realities and moments have been my recurring focus. Now I want to direct my thoughts to the history of my life as the larger world determined my place, my approach, the needs of the day, and the response from people of the time to the issues of the time.

I am now going to write of the beginnings, as well as the present moment, in the history of my priesthood in the Catholic Church in Winona, and in the world. My life as a priest, as a spiritual leader, has been radically directed and challenged by world historical events.

When I was ordained, Winona could no longer pretend to be an isolated little piece of geography in southern Minnesota. The world was quickly shrinking, and the redefinition of involvement in the world for all people was quickly expanding. Communication technology was in its modern-day inception, but it was very effective in opening the world, the world's people, and the spirit, psychology, and spirituality of humanity of that period. My priesthood was changing, and life was changing, and big things were happening. We were all scrambling to know what to do, how to help others to know what to do, in our search for God, for hope, for stability.

When I was ordained on May 27, 1961, the Catholic Church was euphoric because for the first time in American history a Catholic had recently been elected to the Presidency of the United States. John F. Kennedy had been able to cross the invisible religious line of eligibility for public life, and had succeeded in his political aspirations of serving the nation as president and as Catholic. This was a significant moment for America and for the development of the Catholic Church in America.

Now in 2011, as I approach my seventy-sixth birthday and my fiftieth anniversary as a priest, we have elected our first black president, Barack Obama, who competed with a powerful woman, Hilary Clinton, in the Democratic primaries. Their opponents were a long-standing Republican senator and Viet Nam veteran, John McCain and his female running mate, Sarah Palin. This picture gives me hope, because less than a hundred years ago women could not vote, and certainly could not run for public office. Social change in the state, as in the Church, has crept along at a snail's pace, but it has moved. Social evolvement in politics and in religion, as in personal change, is a slow, painful, deliberate, and life-long process.

In the sixties, Americans traveled safely to the moon and back. This redefined the cosmology, psychology, philosophy, and theology of the time. Robert Kennedy and Martin Luther King Jr. were assassinated as they strived for justice for all Americans. The Civil Rights movement was in full swing, trying to bring equality to people of all colors, national backgrounds, and cultural conditions. The Cold War between America and the USSR was a threat to the peace and survival of the world's people.

As time moved on, America and the Catholic Church were changing at an accelerating pace. Pope Paul VI issued the famous (some would say infamous) encyclical, *Humanae Vitae*, that addressed, among other things, the Catholic Church's position on birth control. Within three or four years of the publication

of this encyclical, the sexual mores, the sexual psychology, and the sexual morality of American Catholics changed radically. Catholic lay people grew up
and stopped going to the celibate priest to ask if they
could make decisions regulating the birth of their
children, the number of children they would have.
They began regulating their own sexual thinking and
practices- behaviors that are private to, and significant
for couples as they manage their families and live
their lives. To me this represents another Christian
Reformation. Catholics were beginning to make decisions, assume responsibilities, and determine what
they would accept in terms of the Gospel and the Roman Catholic Church's official teaching. This was a
moment of victory for Catholics. Catholic lay people
became equal partners with the clergy and hierarchy
in determining policy, conviction, commitment and
practice in their day-to-day application of faith, hope
and charity in their lives.

These same years, the late sixties and early seventies, saw the increased use of horribly toxic, life-
maiming illegal drugs. Adolescents were the victims
of these horrible substances. My work as a high
school principal and college director of students
brought me into contact with many painful, tragic stories of drugs in the sixties. Many lives were forever
altered, and family life was very often a victim of

drug use and abuse. Some children lost their futures in that painful and wild time. The young people simply did not know how to handle this challenge. Adults, parents, school personnel, Church leaders, and legal operatives did not know how to get a handle on this moving, dark, illegal, and lethal experience.

Today we still struggle, as a society and as a faith tradition, to address the energies that drive the drug world. Our biggest mistake would be to give up trying to remedy this very difficult social issue which is destroying so many of our youth. Spiritual energy, religious discipline and practice certainly are instruments that we must continue to believe in, to practice, and to offer to the larger community, as at least partial solutions to this socially destructive problem.

In our faith practice we speak of the theological virtues of faith, seeking truth; hope, seeking more and new life; and charity, seeking unity between and among all dimensions of living existence. And we describe the foundational cardinal virtues of prudence, justice, fortitude and temperance as the stable foundation upon which both individual and corporate life can find integrity, stability, and a meaningful direction. As Christians, our role, at least partially in my estimation, is to persevere, to stay the course, to believe in the basic truth of Jesus Christ and of the Gospel that has followed Him, His life and teachings, making His Spirit alive today.

I have remained a priest all these years because I believe what my parents and my Church taught me. That is, that charity, justice, truth, integrity, perseverance, and basic human common sense and dignity are integral aspects of the message of Jesus, and that nothing since His time has surpassed that message. To this I have devoted my life. I believe that God's Spirit is alive and is directing us even now, in the current realities of life.

A new appreciation of the Gospel is needed today, in this age of cell phones, iPods, iPads, and all of the other technological instruments that have become a part of our mind-set. I say this because I am sure they are modifying the psychology, the spirituality of the day. The challenge of the Church today, in my mind, is to stay the course of the Gospel, to continue our basic belief in the foundations of human needs, and to try to offer the truth of life, as offered in the Gospel, to all people.

One of the major challenges of this day in life in America, as we experience it, is to learn how to keep a spiritual stability and foundation, along with intellectual and physical issues that demand attention constantly. Spirituality drives everything else, and without a healthy spirit nothing works as I experience my journey.

I believe deeply that young parents need to give their children a tradition of faith by practicing it themselves, along with their children. Children do not learn primarily through verbal instruction. They learn by watching their parents, by being involved in the practices of their parents, by the milieu in which parents and the children live. We are impacted, in my view, much more deeply and authentically by visions and experiences, and by participating in the activities of family life, than we are by being "told what to do".

I believe that the increase in divorces and the loss of children from their parents is the result of believing that we can think ourselves through problems in family life, in intimate life, in relational life. We are not minds seeking logic. We are human beings seeking peace and unity with the earth, with all of society, with our intimates. We cannot harness emotional energy, and yet emotional energy is what drives us humans in the most important decisions that we make. Emotion and spirit are united in the human heart so profoundly that they dictate the conditions of our lives. Logic is very important for life, but logic is not the leader of life in the vast majority of life experiences.

Emotional health and balance, and spiritual integrity, are the ingredients which lead an individual to peace of mind and happiness. Jesus taught that He was the way, the truth and the life, and the experience of Jesus is not raw logic. Rather, the experience of Jesus and of His message is the fullness of humanity, the social dimension, body, mind, emotion, and spirit.

I feel that I have somewhat failed the people that I have served over fifty years in the sense that sometimes I tried harder to verbally teach them rather than becoming involved with them from day to day to day. Human relationships rather than human logic are what move individuals and societies along in the process of growth and deepening of spirit.

A challenge for all of culture in this present moment is to determine how we can engage the technological world without losing the spiritual dimension of individuals and of society. Our Gospel reminds us that we are human beings before we are technical experts.

Our world has changed radically since 1961, when I was ordained. Our globe, our nation and our person have all been redefined. During those fifty years, racial and sexual barriers have been weakened if not yet completely broken. The Cold War and the increase in nuclear weapons around the world changed the political emphasis of America. Technological development has made it totally impossible for a region or a town to remain in isolation.

The movement from land-based telephone lines to the present cell phone reality has significantly changed our culture. We have gone from "party lines" and other slow and troublesome communication patterns to the ability to instantaneously reach around the world both audibly and visually.

Terrorist movements have totally redefined America's methods of self-defense, as well as its methods of interaction with other nations. Our philosophy of diplomacy has been challenged to reinvestigate every dimension of life at home and around the world. Our politics have been changed in ways that we could never have imagined twenty years ago. Budgetary policies have been changed, and this has touched our social programs for the poor and our emphasis on quality education for all of our children, to name but two of the phases of our society that impact the future of our nation.

Our defense budget has always been a big, disproportionate percent of our finances. We must remain strong as a nation, but we citizens need, in my estimation, to continuously challenge our leaders not to become paranoid, but to serve and develop our citizens educationally and socially. We are failing as a nation in educating our children. Continued ignorance of the need to improve our children's education is a formula for disaster. Knowledge is power, and without power our nation is in trouble.

The continued experience of immigration into this country, which has been the definition of this nation from its inception, has challenged us, especially the Caucasian population, to welcome people from nations from which immigrants have never come before. We are asked to remember that our own ancestors came to America because life in their previous home was difficult, persecuting, frightening, or simply impossible. We today are called to open our hearts, our minds, and our nation to those who differ radically from us in so many aspects of life. But we are asked to remember that they, like our ancestors, are coming to this nation for freedom, for opportunity, for security, for peace. As our ancestors were welcomed (or at least tolerated), so now it is our vocation to reach out to those coming to America, to learn of their histories, to understand their conditions, to assist them to become one with us.

Religious customs, spiritual traditions and moral applications of principle need to be reviewed in terms of these new circumstances. The Gospel of Jesus is perpetual, sound and stable, but its application to each new age demands intelligent thought, broad insight, and courageous wisdom. The Gospel will work today, but only as we apply it to the conditions, the circumstances, and the people of today.

Christian spirituality always demands prayer, reflection, prudence, and thoughtful consideration, as we bring ourselves into the lives and destinies of others. Christian morality is a moving, living, and demanding art and science, as it is fitted to the new, challenging, changing, and growing phenomena of each new day. Morality demands thoughtfulness. The difficult moral issues of our day demand courage, communion, communication, truth, tradition, humility, and persevering consideration of the realities of our lives.

Homosexuality

A significant experience in my life as a priest was when I began to learn about gay and lesbian people, as they began to "come out of the closet," slowly at first, about forty or forty-five years ago. After the success of the civil rights movement and the slow dismantling of racism, other social realities began to emerge, and sexual prejudice toward gay and lesbian people became more explicit, more demeaning and angry. Also, the gay and lesbian people slowly began to come together, to find their voice, and to begin to form systems that could help and empower them to assist each other and their families. Gay and lesbian people found their own dignity, and began to systematically develop confidence in their ability and responsibility to change the secretive, demeaning and negative approach to themselves and to their orientation by much of society. This, as is the case for many other social movements, was to be a bumpy road.

Medical science has shown homosexuality to be a biological reality, through much research, study, and involvement with the gay community. People do not choose to be heterosexual or homosexual, but much of our heterosexual society finds it extremely difficult to trust the biological facts of this issue. Sexual prejudice, like racial or religious prejudice, runs deep in our culture.

Over the years I have spent many, many hours with gay and lesbian people, one on one, in counseling. Their inability or unwillingness to accept their situation as gay was a big hurdle for many of the good people I spoke with. Their fear of the reaction of their families, if they came out as gay, was also very frightening for many. Many were afraid of losing jobs, of being blocked from professional advancements, and of being demeaned and harassed at work if they told the truth of their sexual orientation.

Many Catholic people would utilize the Sacrament of Reconciliation to discuss this matter because they felt safer with the seal of confession involved. The seal of confession means that the priest may never speak about anything that is discussed in the Sacrament of Reconciliation, and also the priest is excused from having to testify in any court regarding what is discussed and confessed in the sacrament by a penitent.

Over the years I have been privileged to lead family meetings with gay members who decided to inform their families of their sexual orientation. Usually these meetings went fairly well, but were often difficult and tearful for one or another member of the family. On a few occasions a family member would totally reject the gay member, and this was always very painful for all involved. Most of the time, as the years went by, reconciliation between estranged family members slowly took place, as all involved could come to an acceptance of the gay issue.

Over the years significant numbers of gay and lesbian Catholics have expressed privately to me, and more and more publicly in the secular press, how disillusioned they have become with the Catholic Church and its official teachings. Their message generally is that the Gospel teaching of the Church is universal love, respect for person and for life, forgiveness, acceptance of people in their differences, and a welcoming inclusion. On the other hand, the gay and lesbian community feels excluded, ostracized, demeaned, lectured to and dismissed, especially by the hierarchy of the Catholic Church. Gays and lesbians, in my experience, are very angry about the sexual abuse of children at the hands of priests, and about the manner in which the hierarchy generally has handled this scandal, usually in the setting of secrecy, legal defense of Church power and property, and the paying of millions of dollars in settlements. Many gay Catholics have left our Church, partly because they perceive that the hierarchy is unwilling to dialogue with them about their issues.

An experience I had about fifteen years ago, in trying to help some gay and lesbian people bring their message, their concerns, and their fears to the public, sticks in my mind. A gay man, who had been a priest and a friend of mine, had left the priesthood. Some years later he called me and asked if I would come to a panel presentation which was to address the gay and lesbian issue and presence in the Church. I assured him that I would be present.

The program consisted of a panel of six people, all of them gay or lesbian. Each was to speak for six to eight minutes, and then the floor would be opened to dialogue, discussion and questions. The gay participants included a Catholic priest, a Catholic religious sister, a Lutheran female minister, two lay men and one lay woman.

The panel members each gave clear, respectful observations about being gay, the reactions of other people toward them, and the struggles involved as they tried to understand and live their lives. When they had finished speaking the floor was opened for audience participation. The first speaker to get up was a priest much younger than I. He attacked the panelists for their comments, made some very inappropriate accusations, and lectured all present on the official teaching of the Catholic Church on homosexuality.

I knew that I, as one of very few Catholic priests present, had to respond to the former speaker's comments. I rose, asked the Chair for permission to speak, and said something like, "I was ordained in 1961, and for the next five to seven years, priests in southeast Minnesota heard confessions for hours every Saturday of the year. The matters confessed were almost exclusively sexual- specifically, artificial birth control. This pattern of very heavy confessions every week lasted until two or three years after Pope Paul VI issued the encyclical entitled *Humanae Vitae*. The encyclical spoke about human dignity in all forms and dimensions, and reiterated the Catholic position on artificial birth control. I do not understand what happened, but within two to three years of *Humanae Vitae* being promulgated, the confessions fell off radically. Today, in 2011, one priest in our largest parishes will hear confessions for thirty to forty minutes per week. People came to know that they also had the Holy Spirit, and they found the confidence needed to decide what their sexual behaviors, dignity and practices would be. No longer did many people come to ask the priest about their sexual life." I further observed that I believed that the current moment in which I was addressing this panel and this audience was a new opportunity to address respectfully and thoroughly this entire issue of homosexuality, which was beginning to emerge in our culture.

Early the next day after this panel experience I received a call from the Bishop's office, insisting that I tell them what I had said publicly the night before at that panel. I was not told who had called and reported me, but I knew who he was. I answered their questions truthfully, was reminded by the chancery official on the other end of the phone line how important it is to be prudent when speaking publicly, and we hung up. I at that moment understood much better how the gay community feels around the official hierarchical Church.

The depth of this prejudice toward gay members in our society has been proven again constantly by the continuing debate in our national government concerning gay people serving in the military. For so long we Americans have had a law on our books called, "Don't ask, don't tell" concerning gay people who were serving in uniform, or gay people who wanted to serve in uniform for our nation. Stories are constantly being reported on the national news about prejudice toward gays in the military. Occasionally, these stories have been disastrous for a gay military person.

To this point in my life, we have begun to study the biology, the psychology, the sociology, the spirituality, and the morality of the homosexual question, but we, as a Church and a society, have a long way to go in addressing this issue. As education continues to advance, and as the knowledge explosion on our planet continues to accelerate, we are becoming aware frequently of new moral issues which engage us, and with which we must deal. Homosexuality is one of those issues, and it is a frightening one for much of our society. People depend on the Church to give calm, truthful and directive information on these issues. To date the Church has sent mixed messages on the issue of homosexuality.

It is common knowledge in the ranks of the priests of this country that many of our number are gay and they are good priests. Rome and the bishops insist that gay people are not welcome in the priesthood. No one has the ability to know who is gay and who is heterosexual, as young men enter the seminary. No one has the right to plunder another person's conscience as to personal intent and direction on this or any other issue.

It seems to me that we are homophobic in our approach to homosexuality as it relates to the priesthood because we have not honestly dealt with this issue to date in our Church. We continue to struggle with this issue.

Abortion

A few times in my fifty years as a priest I have been scolded by lay people because they think that I do not speak out forcefully enough against abortion. I have responded, as best I could when this accusation spontaneously occurred, that I, as a confessor to all people, choose not to overload any sin or failure regarding our Catholic moral teaching because the parishioners with whom I deal on a daily basis are sometimes the participants in this or that particular failure and experience.

I will never forget the experience that I had with a woman in her fifties who rather aggressively attacked me, somewhat publicly, for not being hard enough on abortion in my preaching. I attempted to tell her that people out there in the congregation have experienced this reality and are suffering from guilt, secrecy, and shame for their decision, and that I did not want to add to this pain for them. Her response was that they did what they did and had to pay for it. She did not know then, and never will know, that her daughter, a wonderful young woman, was one of the people that I had been dealing with in counseling and in sacramental experience for some months.

In our day, abortion has been singled out for particular emphasis, both religiously and culturally, by the so-called "pro-life" people. Never once in fifty years have I heard a grassroots statement against the capital punishment laws of this country by those who profess to be pro-life. Our Church teaches that we must not kill. Rarely have I heard a statement against our governmental policies that have taken us into wars that kill innocent civilians (this carnage being explained away as "collateral damage"). Never have I heard a radical pro-life person complain about the policies in this country that exclude up to one-fourth of our population from adequate health care. In my understanding of the Gospel, all of these, as well as other dimensions of life, are subject to the moral

teachings of Jesus, as the twenty-first century inter-
prets that teaching.

I am continually taught by these circumstances
and relationships not to judge opinions, but also never
to cave in to pressure by the vocal members of our
Church tradition who are sincere, but who see or
choose to look at only ten percent of the moral picture. Abortion is wrong, no question! No argument!
But it is one moral issue among many others that demand our collective attention as a teaching and learning Church.

In our world of internet and instantaneous
communication, we are told every day that knowledge
is exploding in dimensions that we have not experienced before, and that we do not completely know
how to handle. The challenge for our Church, for the
people of God, is to humbly, and in a disciplined
manner, dialogue about how to address the unfolding
of knowledge, the exposing of new issues, the unroll-
ing of new moral problems. We cannot serve humanity by being a one-issue Church, a one-focused community, or a one dimensional moral teacher. We must
heed the many voices that say we should continue to
unfold, to open our senses, to anticipate new dimensions of life, to keep our minds open and alert to the
possible realities that continuously appear on the horizon of human experience and study.

CHAPTER 27

Listening

When I was in college at Immaculate Heart of Mary Seminary, located on the campus of Saint Mary's University in Winona, one of my classmates asked a professor, who was a priest, "What is the one most important tool a priest needs in order to help people?" The professor answered, "You need a big back end and an open ear." The year was 1957.

The professor went on to say that people have a definite and deep need to be listened to. And he told us that a significant part of the role of the priest is to listen to people, especially hurting, frightened, guilty and grieving, depressed, wounded people. Fifty years as a priest have affirmed the truth of that statement made so many years ago. I have had to learn to listen, listen, and listen. People may ask advice, but people certainly do need to be listened to.

Sacramental listening for the priest is to listen to confessions, and offer the absolution of our Church.

I am certain that I have listened to 50,000 confessions in fifty years as a priest. That would compute out as approximately eighty-three confessions each month, or about three each day.

I have listened to confessions in barns, in very poor homes, and in mansions. I have listened to confessions of powerful people, a couple of famous people, and people who will spend the entirety of their lives in prison. I have listened to the confession of a few professional athletes. Our humanity is beautiful, but also sometimes weak, and always fallible. Listening to confessions has always been a profound privilege for me. It is difficult work because it demands the best attention that I can give. Active listening is not child's play. Active listening is demanding. It is healing for the person being listened to.

In my priesthood I know that I have listened for at least 25,000 hours to people whose marriages were coming apart, who were experiencing trouble with their adolescent or young adult children, to people whose health is failing, to youngsters who are pregnant out of wedlock, to people who are very embarrassed about public disclosure of their faults, to spouses who have just learned that their partner is unfaithful to them, and the list goes on.

I have listened for hundreds of hours to people who suffer from depression, and who are embarrassed about that fact. It has taken, sometimes, years of listening before some depressed persons find the courage to address the issue medically and with family and friends. Depression is another experience of society that has a long way to go, as we try to assist each other. This reality has been for me as a priest perhaps the single most difficult human experience to deal with, as I listen to hurting people.

Pain, guilt, disappointment, fear, bewilderment, anxiety, depression, failure at personal expectations, and relational tensions of all kinds, bring people to their pastor or priest for comfort, for direction, for advice, and for reassurance for the current issue before them. The human spirit, personality, and identity must be cared for, nurtured, and renewed as much as the body needs to be fed, toileted, bathed and exercised. I believe that listening is the main function, experience, and practice for a person to continue to be balanced, healthy, and happy and at peace in mind, body and spirit. I also believe that when this balance is lost through some traumatic experience, listening is the main ingredient for renewed peace, hope and life.

A very extensive part of my life has been invested in listening to others. This reality in my youngest years as a priest used to be more of a challenge to me because I did not think I was doing any good. The practice and perseverance in listening, however, taught me that perhaps, on a one-to-one basis, listening is the most important gift that I could offer. I have no doubt today that listening to hurting people has been one of the most significant aspects of my life journey and gift to others.

The following story is true, and has touched me very deeply. About a year ago I had a flat tire about noon on a Sunday. I pulled off the main thoroughfare, and began to try to change the tire. The bolts on the wheel had been secured by machine, and were so tightly secured that I was not strong enough to loosen them. I called my two brothers, Richard and Bernard, who were at Richard's farm near Chatfield, Minnesota. I explained my situation, and they said that they would come to help me, but that it would be at least a half-hour before they could get to me.

I was standing by my automobile, waiting for my brothers to arrive when, all of a sudden, an old rusted-out and noisy car pulled around the corner and parked in front of me. Two young Hispanic men, approximately twenty-one years of age, jumped out of their car and came toward me saying, "We want to change your tire." They were dressed in clean clothes, so I said that I did not want them to get dirty.

They said that they had just been at their niece's baptism, and that they were on their way to the party at the home of her parents to celebrate this big day for their family. I said, "Please, don't get all dirty for your niece's party." They said that they would not get dirty, but that they wanted to change my tire. I relented. They began, very efficiently, to change the tire. As they were doing so, one of the young men said to me, "Do you remember me?" I replied that I had been looking at him, wondering where I had met him, but I could not remember.

He said to me, "You met me in jail." And immediately I remembered him. He had been arrested on an alcohol charge, and ended up in jail for a few weeks. He had been so embarrassed and sad that he had let his family down. I offer Mass twice a month at the Olmsted County Jail. It was at one of those Masses that I had met this young man. He stayed around after the Mass to talk. I listened to him on a few occasions, and then he left jail, and I assumed that I would never see him again.

On the day of the flat tire, after we talked for a while he said to me, "I told my cousin that we had to help you out because you had helped me so much in jail, and I wanted to repay you." All I had done for this young man was to listen to him seriously and attentively. He remembered that fact, and when he saw me in need, he came to pay back. The moral of this story is that listening sincerely heals, strengthens, and inspires. I was, and am, deeply touched by this memory.

Another experience, and profound teacher, is to listen to people who are near death. I have mentioned this sort of experience previously in this work, but would like to enlarge upon it here. I have had the privilege of sitting at the bedside of hundreds, probably more than a thousand, people who were approaching death. This time of our existence has a unique character. A person has never been there before, has no experience as to what to expect. One is facing the end of life as she or he has known it, saying goodbye to loved ones, to possessions, to unrealized dreams.

A person in this setting is facing the ultimate mystery of his or her existence. It appears to me that the dying process brings each of us to the most authentic, humble, accepting, and realistic moments of our entire journey as conscious human beings. There remains no room for negotiating, the patient is not in charge, and has nothing to say about whether she or he will die. The only decision, if the patient is conscious, is how to die, how to surrender, how to let go of all that one has clung to throughout life on the earth.

The death process is a profound privilege to family members, pastors, doctors, nurses, and for all people who deal with the dying patient. Listening at this point of the journey of any human being is a blessing for the dying person and for those who participate in this moment. To listen now is to bless, to be present, to support, and to reassure the dying person and the self that we live in faith, we live in mystery, and we live as gifted, vulnerable creatures before our God.

The listening for all of us does not terminate at the death of the patient. Her or his gift to survivors is that the deceased person has taught us a bit better how to listen to each other. Listening negates wars, listening solves family problems, listening is the strongest tool, in my opinion, for a government in governing, in diplomacy, in international relations. Listening is the foundation of peace, justice, and love.

Perhaps the greatest benefit of listening, for the listener, is that this stance, behavior, and practice takes away my ego. Listening asks me to be about the person to whom I am listening. Listening puts my agenda in second place for a while. Listening is a discipline that deepens the character of the listener, that neutralizes the tendency to be selfish, and redirects the energy of life from me to the other. This is a balancing act that is essential to my spiritual, mental, psychological and social health. I know that my life has been deepened, enriched immensely, and given new directions because my work brought me, almost daily for the last fifty years, to the place of listening to some-one who was hurting, afraid, vulnerable, guilty, de-pressed, discouraged, or just in need at that moment in life to have someone listen and pay attention.

Loneliness is a companion to each of us some-time in life. Loneliness is a frequent companion to the less fortunate people- to those who are uneducated, to those who are mentally ill, to those who are socially inept, to those who have suffered and/or carry handi-caps, physical, mental, emotional, or social.

Loneliness needs to be treated gently, sincerely, and continuously. A great contribution to society and to individuals is the simple willingness to stop, pay attention to the person, and listen. This has been a constant part of my life as a priest. Many poor people who have marriage problems come to the priest for help and advice because they cannot afford a coun-selor. Many people who have family problems come to the priest because they cannot afford professional help. Many family members who have addicted spouses, children, siblings or parents, come to the priest for financial reasons. People who have been publicly embarrassed come to the priest because they believe that he will not further embarrass them.

The fact that our Catholic tradition of faith has made listening a sacramental reality in the Sacrament of Confession, or as we now call it, Reconciliation, speaks volumes to me about the importance of listening. I have, thousands of times, experienced the comfort that it gives to the person who comes to confession. This service of hearing confessions for others is one of the greatest rewards I receive as a priest, because people are so grateful to be able to safely and confidentially unburden their heart and their conscience of whatever the current or remembered issue might be.

I have come to know that no issue that disturbs a person is unimportant. For the person bearing the issue, it is a thorn and a burden. I, the listener, can alleviate that burden by sincerely, attentively, and in a humble welcoming fashion pay attention to him or her and become involved in the miracle that listening makes happen.

SECTION VII

FINAL
REFLECTIONS

CHAPTER 28

Traveling

I have not written about the travels of my life. Traveling has certainly made a profound impact on who I am, on what I try to do, on how I see life for all of us. I have mentioned earlier in these pages that on June 24, 1990, my sister-in-law, Linda Siskow Nelson, died of cancer, leaving my brother Richard with four children. Beginning that year, and for the next six years, I took my brother's van and the four kids and headed out to the various parts of this country. In the six years that followed, the four kids and I spent two weeks of each year seeing the United States. The children today, now adults, retain fond memories of these trips, as do I.

I have traveled to Hawaii, Mexico, Canada and Alaska. I have traveled to Europe four times, seeing England, France, Germany, Switzerland, Austria, Italy, and the Netherlands. I enjoyed a cruise in the Baltic Sea that took my traveling companions and me to

Denmark, Germany, Estonia, Russia, Sweden, and
Finland. I cruised with friends to the Panama Canal,
visiting several places on the journey.

Traveling has been for me a deep spiritual experience, as I saw how other people lived, perceived
life, and contributed to life in their respective settings.
Traveling opened my eyes, my imagination, my mind,
and my soul to others in a way that no other experience could give. For me, to feel their place, their setting, their culture, and their spirit was a transforming
spiritual experience. My prayer life has been deepened and broadened by the experience of travel.

Travel taught me to address the fears of the un-
known, to welcome new dimensions of life, and to be
open to exchanging life, ideas, philosophies and cultures very different from my own. My spiritual journey has been enriched by many surprising things,
people, and experiences. The entirety of God's creation is a sacred reality which contributes to every person as we open ourselves to new possibilities.

As I grow older and am traveling less, I reflect
on, think about, and ponder the experiences I had in
traveling. That is a beautiful prayer and meditation.
Opening my experience through travel helped open
my mind and spirit, and that is the way that God has
expanded my vision, my perception, my desire to
bring in new people, new life, new possibilities, new

religions, new philosophies, and new dimensions of being in my own faith journey. In this sense, life has been the greatest travel experience of all for me. Geography, sociology, and differing cultures have all enriched my life, but my life itself has been the reality that has placed me where I am, in a very happy, successful, and peaceful situation. My prayer is, "Praise God!"

CHAPTER 29

My Mother's Diary

As I close my own efforts to offer some insights into my life through these memoirs, I am reminded of my mother's diary. For my twelfth birthday my aunt and godmother Gert gave me a diary. I remember my mother telling relatives and friends, throughout all of the years, that Paul faithfully kept the diary for two weeks. And that was and is the truth. At age twelve, a scholar I was not!

However, as I laid the pen down on the diary, my mother picked it up, and I believe that she made an entry in the diary every day of her life, from early June of 1947 until two or three days before her death at the Chatfield Minnesota Chosen Valley Care Center on February 11, 2007. That diary covers a span of time only days short of sixty years. She also kept a careful watch on her farm home. She recorded, for all who want to know, when each calf and colt, puppy, and broods of cats, chickens, ducks and turkeys were brought to life. We have recorded in her diary when the crops were planted and when they were harvested. We have a history of the yield from each crop harvested. We have a history of the weather, especially the dramatic moments of weather, throughout all of the years.

My history, and that of my brothers and of their children and grandchildren, my parents, and of our extended family, are recorded as well. Her records establish a very accurate picture of life for the Nelson-O'Connell family, close relatives, friends and neighbors. Her diary is truly a beautiful record and history of our family's contributions to life in southeastern Minnesota.

As I have reached seventy-six years of age and have experienced fifty plus years serving as a priest, I am finding that my prayer is not so much for the future. My spiritual experience is largely focused on memories, meanings, surprises and questions. What has been the meaning of life? What have I contributed? What difference have I made? How can I assist those younger than myself to make their lives rich, meaningful, happy and fulfilling?

Is the world and human life better because I have been here? How has my contribution helped, enhanced, and contributed to the life of humanity? I reflect on my (our) responsibility as Mother's family, to share these records, these reflections, these accounts of what happened throughout the years. Those who come after us can be enriched by knowing and reflecting on my mother's history, our generation's history, and the movements of our next generation.

We are living in an information age. No information is more important to the family than what has happened to our ancestors, how they experienced life, what they contributed to life, and how they appreciated the life of their day. These are blood truths, family truths, important truths for our progeny.

This approach to life has been for me a wonderful guide, a peaceful experience, a good teacher for the next phase of life. As I have learned to listen to my life in all of its dimensions- its strengths, its weaknesses, its successes, and its failures- I have found peace of mind. As I have learned to own all of the days and experiences of life I have found more control, more self-acceptance, more openness to let my life be what my life has been. I am who I am, no more, no less, no better, no worse!

I am comfortable to know what I believe. I am made in God's image and therefore I am very good. I am also a fallible and imperfect human being, and I need redemption, as do all of my brothers and sisters. That truth does not demean me, disappoint me, trouble me, or discourage me. Life is what it is and my life is what it is, and that is the reality in which I find meaning, direction, significance, determination and hope. Life is, and has been for me, a profound gift. *Deo Gratias*!

Raisa, Salley and Dusty

As I am concluding the writing of my memoirs, I continue to reflect, to remember, to evaluate, to ponder the persons, the experiences, the joys and the sorrows which have formed my life. I have written about much of that energy, but I have come to know in these last few days of writing that I have not written about a very powerful and important piece of my journey for the last twenty years.

That piece of history involves Raisa and Salley, my miniature poodles who were my constant companions for the last twenty years. Having grown up on a farm, I was involved with, and loved animals all of my life. In my younger years as a priest, I either lived with some other priest or priests, or I had young assistants living with me. I know that not all people like animals sharing their space, their living quarters and their lives, so I never considered having a dog.

When I finished my eight year term as Rector of the Cathedral of the Sacred Heart in Winona in

June of 1991, Bishop Vlazny reassigned me to St. Joseph Parish in Owatonna, Minnesota, and I knew that I would be living alone. I immediately began to research dogs, their habits, and their trainability. I concluded that female poodles were among the most intelligent and trainable dogs. Poodles do not shed their fur, and that was important to me because I lived in a parish rectory, and did not want to have a dog that would shed a lot of hair there.

During July of 1991 I searched for a miniature female poodle. I found one in Minneapolis, Minnesota. I called the breeder and agreed to buy my first dog as a priest. I was told that the little dog that I had bought, sight unseen, was a silver-haired and shy poodle. I was told that she was very intelligent and well house trained. All of that information was true.

The day that I drove from Owatonna to Minneapolis to accept my dog was, I believe, August 23, 1991. It was a Saturday and I left Owatonna after my 4:00 PM Mass to travel to pick up the dog. All the way to the Twin Cities, as I drove, the radio was reporting the fall of the former USSR. Russia had fallen and had come apart that day, and, of course, this was the news of the world. The news commentators were speaking repeatedly about the fact that Mikhail and Raisa Gorbachev had been detained in their country home because of the unrest in Moscow.

I was thinking all the way to the Twin Cities of a name for the dog. As I heard the reports on the leaders of Russia, Mikhail and Raisa, I made the decision to name my dog Raisa, after the Russian First Lady. That proved to be a great decision, and a source of having to tell the story of my dog's name almost every day of her life for the next ten years.

Raisa was a wonderful and shy little poodle. She was gentle but distant to people who approached her. She and I were very close, and had a wonderful life together for almost ten years. I did have to tell people hundreds of times why her name was Raisa. It was a joyful and interesting time. Raisa developed a serious problem with her hips at age ten and began to suffer much, so I made a very difficult decision to have Raisa put down in the spring of 2000.

In the fall of 2000 I was ready for another poodle. I found Salley, as a puppy, in Prairie du Chein, Wisconsin. Salley got her name because we live on Salley Lane, N.W. in Rochester. She was an exciting and friendly little puppy. And she has proven to be the finest, friendliest and most sociable dog in the city of Rochester. She is now eleven years old. She has been in our parish school at St. Pius X. She has attended Mass at St. Pius X. Salley has been the star of the show at many wedding rehearsals and at many baptisms at St. Pius X. She has gone to rest homes with me in Rochester and Chatfield. She was present for my fiftieth anniversary celebration at St. Pius X, and she greeted all the people who came. She loves little children and older adults. Salley is known to most of the people of St. Pius X. Parish. She regularly wanders through the church before Mass begins or after Mass has ended. She knows exactly where the little children sit during Mass because there are always Cheerios on the floor in those locations. Salley has attended several coffee and doughnut Sundays in Kennedy Hall and she has also been at several monthly pancake breakfasts in Kennedy Hall.

She and I have not missed our daily walk very many days in the last eleven years. Only a few bitter cold days each year have stopped us from our walk. About ten years ago, while I still lived in Austin and served as pastor of St. Augustine Parish, Salley awakened me in the middle of the night very dramatically, barking loudly. I let her out of my second floor apartment and she ran swiftly down the stairs to the back door of the rectory and broke up an attempted break-in. Two men had almost destroyed the back door, when she and I got there to scare them off.

Salley has been a spiritual companion for me. We live together all the time. She travels with me in the car most of the time. She sleeps at the foot of my bed. Salley tells me when she needs to go outside. She

PAUL NELSON

has been and is, in a sense, my soul mate. We are certainly one in spirit. Salley has taught me repeatedly that God is present in all of God's creatures.

During many of the years when Salley was my constant companion, I also dog-sat another little four-pound male poodle named Dusty. Dusty belonged to very good friends. He liked me and Salley, and was totally comfortable in my home. Dusty, in spite of his small stature, was the "alpha dog," the boss of any place he chose to inhabit. He was a delight to have around, sometimes a nuisance, occasionally a marker of my furniture, always good for a laugh. If I were to pick him up, and he was not in the mood to be held, he would gently put his small mouth around one of my fingers, touching his teeth to my skin, but never once biting me. He just seemed to have the "small dog syndrome" enough to want to let me know who really was in charge. He would look at me as if to say, "Watch it!" He is the little dog that I am holding along with Salley in one of the pictures in this memoir. These little poodles have truly enriched my life for the past twenty-plus years.

CHAPTER 30

Reflections on My Fiftieth Anniversary of Ordination

As I write this evening (May 28, 2011), I am nostalgic, because yesterday was my fiftieth anniversary of ordination to the priesthood in the Roman Catholic tradition of Christianity. I was ordained on May 27, 1961, by Bishop Edward A. Fitzgerald at the Cathedral of the Sacred Heart in Winona, Minnesota. After being ordained on that morning, the bishop and my classmates and I met in the basement of the Cathedral to have lunch. It was about 12:30 PM. Each of us knew where we were to sit, because an envelope with our name on it was resting on our lunch plates. As we gathered around the table, Bishop Fitzgerald said, "Do not open those envelopes until I tell you to do so."

We said a prayer over our food, sat down, and it was then that the bishop told us to open our envelopes. Each of the envelopes contained a first assignment as a priest. He then directed that we should take our turns, and report to each other where we had been assigned to begin our work. When my turn came, I read that I was to serve as an Assistant Pastor at Saint Augustine Parish in Austin, Minnesota, and that I was assigned to teach Religion on a full-time basis at Pacelli High School in Austin.

I was delighted with the assignment because the pastor at Saint Augustine Parish, Msgr. Robert Jennings, was known in the diocese as being one of the kindest pastors to whom assistants were assigned. I also liked the challenge of teaching high school students, even though I had experienced only three days of practice teaching in my college years. Needless to say, I was scared to death, but determined to give my best to this effort.

This assignment defined my life, although I did not know that to be the case that nervous afternoon. To teach high school students demanded that I prepare for each class thoroughly, that I do very accurate research in that preparation, and that I develop a style of presentation in the classroom that would keep me in charge of a class of thirty-five students while at the same time not coming off as a dictator or as an arrogant person. High school students have a sixth sense as to the spirit of their teachers. Somehow I knew that truth, and was able to negotiate those turbulent waters quite well.

Because I prepared each day very thoroughly, and because I worked very hard, I was a very good high school teacher. The students responded to me well, and my principal gave me very positive reviews when he watched me teach. I spent three years teaching juniors at Pacelli. I taught five classes a day, with approximately thirty-five students in each class. During the summers of this assignment I attended St. Mary's University to study for a Masters Degree in Educational Administration.

At the end of three years, Bishop Fitzgerald reassigned me to Winona. I was to serve in the Diocesan Office of Education part-time, as teacher of Religion for two hours every school day at Cotter High School, and help out at St. John's Parish on the east end of Winona on the weekends. This assignment lasted one year.

Early in May of 1965, as I was finishing my fourth year as a priest, Bishop Fitzgerald asked me how much work I had to finish to qualify for the Masters degree in Educational Administration. I told him that all of my course work had been accomplished, but that I needed to write the thesis. He told me to get it done that summer because he was appointing me to be Principal of Cotter High School the following fall.

Cotter was a school of over 650 students and a staff of over sixty full- and part-time people. I needed the degree to meet accrediting standards of the North Central Accrediting Agency, which accredited Cotter.

So that summer found me working sixteen and sometimes more hours a day, in order to finish that thesis and to learn the ropes at Cotter. My farm upbringing stood me in good stead, because I knew how to work and how to persevere and how to stay relatively calm through this challenge. Apparently, my superiors saw some ability in me for them to assign me to this very responsible position at such a young and inexperienced age.

I went on to spend ten very happy and successful years at Cotter as the principal. Cotter taught me more than I gave to Cotter, but that period of my priesthood was in many ways the happiest time of my life. I have never had a bad assignment and have always been happy in my work, but the Cotter years were the frosting on the cake. That assignment and experience defined my entire priesthood. Throughout my life I have been given big assignments, assignments that demanded focus, judgment, deliberation, and determination. I am very thankful to say that I was successful in all of the assignments I ever received.

I left Cotter to become Superintendent of the Catholic Schools for the Diocese of Winona while at the same time serving as the Principal of Loyola High School in Mankato. The latter assignment lasted only a year, the bishop then reassigning me to Austin Pacelli as principal, as that institution was experiencing some serious social and legal issues. The bishop told me that I had more experience with the business of the school than anyone else, so off I went to Austin for the second time. After three years, Pacelli had settled down, and the bishop appointed me to serve as pastor of Queen of Angels Parish in Austin, one of the largest parishes in the diocese.

Less than one week after I arrived at Queen of Angels, my father died. This was a very difficult, emotional, and challenging moment for me. But with the help of many people I survived this experience and grew from the death of my dad. The mystery of Jesus Christ took on new dimensions for me at that time, because I came to realize experientially that God's Holy Spirit was present in life and in death. Nothing escapes God's Spirit, and that realization was extremely clear to me at that moment.

My father's death helped me redefine my approach to suffering and death. Somehow I came to appreciate the fact that in life, in success, in suffering, in diminishment and death, in all of these human experiences and moments, God is present. The wisdom of life comes in surprising packages, and at inopportune moments, but if I could keep myself alert, I could and did grow immensely, through my father's dying process. Again, I did not know what was happening to me at that moment, as a human being, as a son, as a priest. But I was changed in a way that enabled me, for all the years to come, to be present to, to share grief with, and to process the movement of family life as one member of the family leaves through the doors of death. Dad's death launched me into the current of emotion, realization of the finality of death, and into the continuing adjustment that life demands of us, sometimes through success and progress, sometimes through failure and death. Life gives us health of body, mind, and spirit if we open ourselves to the experience, to the change, to the reality of the present moment.

As I recall the date of my father's death, June 28, 1977, I realize that I came to a deeper and richer appreciation of the mystery of death as it touches every family. When death comes, predictably or surprisingly, it changes our perceptions, our emotions, our convictions, and our life directions as we currently understand them. Part of this change came for me through the confusion, the depression, the loss, the relationship with my mother and brothers, through the activities of the next several days, as we met with the mortician, as we planned the funeral, and as we experienced the wake, the funeral Mass and the burial of Dad's body at St. Bridget's cemetery near Simpson, Minnesota. The direction of our lives as a family had shifted, and we needed to learn the new direction of life for each of us, if we hoped to be happy mentally, emotionally, and spiritually. I came to a new appreciation that this is the experience and the process and the possibility for every family as they experience death.

I have had a wonderful life of challenge, joy, opportunity, and accomplishment. I served as principal at three of the four of our diocesan high schools, Winona Cotter for ten years, Mankato Loyola for one year, and Austin Pacelli for three years. I have also served as pastor of four of the largest parishes in our diocese- Queen of Angels in Austin for six years, Cathedral of the Sacred Heart in Winona for eight years, St. Joseph in Owatonna for two years, and St. Augustine in Austin for ten years. For the last eight years I have happily served as the Associate Pastor of St. Pius X Parish in Rochester. I have had fifty plus years of the happiest life one could imagine. I am humbly grateful.

My assignments have been very challenging, and happily so. Never was an assignment overwhelm-

ing, but always I was pushed to fulfill something beyond comfort. It appears that I need to live on the
margin, that I enjoy being challenged, that life is a
further invitation to contribute, to participate in, and
to investigate possibilities every day. Again, I believe
that my farm background gave me the strength, the
curiosity, the perseverance, and the social awareness
that has served me well throughout my fifty-plus
years as a priest.

Today, May 29, 2011, I drove with my pastor,
Father Charlie Collins, to Sherburn, Minnesota to
celebrate the fiftieth anniversary of my closest life
friend and classmate, Father Charles Quinn. He invited us to participate in the Mass of his celebration.
Approximately five hundred people were present at
St. Luke's Catholic Church in Sherburn for the Mass.
I met Charles Quinn in September of 1953, as we
walked into the Immaculate Heart of Mary Seminary
located on the campus of St. Mary's University in Winona. We were about to begin studying for the Diocesan Priesthood of the Church of the Diocese of Winona. We have been best friends for all of the past
fifty-eight years. We have spent vacations together,
we have traveled together locally and abroad, we have
taken retreats together, and we have shared mutual
friends over all the years.

278

This day has been very reflective for me in that I was reminded that I also have had fifty years as a priest, serving people in Austin, Winona, Mankato, Owatonna, Rochester, and surrounding areas. My life has not primarily been about me. It has been about us, God's people, serving, helping, forgiving, loving, renewing, encouraging and nurturing each other the best we could. This is the Gospel of Jesus Christ. This is what we believe and try our best to live, although we know that we do not live the Gospel perfectly. Next weekend, I will celebrate the fifty years of my journey at St. Pius X Church with many of the people I have shared with over the years.

Today was a celebration of fifty years of life for Charles Quinn and the thousands of people with whom he interacted in all of those years, which involved many communities in southern Minnesota. Our lives are lived out with and for each other. Our Christian call is to live the life we have been given to the best of our ability, with generosity and care for the others who come into our lives.

Priestly life is about leading people into mystery, into sacrament, into word, into community, and into wisdom. The mystery of God and of existence, the sacraments of our faith tradition, the word that we reflect on every time we worship, and the community that we perpetually try to build through charity, patience, forgiveness and sharing with each other, are the elements of our faith journey. These activities and attitudes are the Spirit of God alive in each of us and in all of us together. This is the spirit that makes the Christ live among us. Each of us is responsible for contributing to that reality.

I celebrated my seventy-sixth birthday on May 24, 2011, and my fiftieth anniversary of priesthood on May 27, 2011. This observance has given me a new perspective on the life that I enjoy. Dramatically, I have come to realize that my life is mostly behind me. My future on this planet is limited. The psychology and spirituality of this realization have given me pause. I am trying to come to terms with what every aging person must deal with, that is our mortality. Success, planning for the future, determining new plans for structures, setting new goals for the long range of our lives, have been transformed into focusing on the reality of limited time for my living, on spiritual concepts that have driven my life, on changing perspectives which empower me every day, and on studying a totally new dimension of existence leading me to the end of my earthly life and career. Living the spirituality and psychology of this period of my life takes me down a new and inexperienced road. I truly learn this path by walking it.

CHAPTER 31

My Fiftieth Anniversary Celebration

Since the last section was written, I have been given my own celebration! On Saturday, June 4th and Sunday, June 5th 2011, I celebrated the fiftieth anniversary of my priesthood ordination. After all four Masses at St. Pius X Church that weekend, over fifteen hundred people came to the receptions to offer congratulations, gifts, thanks, greetings of affection and respect. I am humbled and overwhelmed by this spirit, so genuinely offered by so many people of all ages.

I learned again, and intensely, how important it is to give people a chance to express the emotion that surrounds the important moments and experiences in their faith lives. A big piece of the significance of the priesthood is that the priest represents the mystery of God and the entire community in validating, celebrating, observing and marking these significant moments for individuals and for families. I learned that weekend in a new way that families need to mark certain moments in their journeys through religious and spiritual expressions, and they need and want to verbally express their souls to the priest. This is and was a most humbling, gratifying and rewarding experience.

The soul of us humans is experienced in, and expressed through, the stories of our respective journeys. The Gospel is powerful because it teaches through stories. Family traditions grow, develop and become solid for future generations through the stories of the family members. Jesus never theorized. Jesus told and listened to stories. Stories reveal the truth about life, love, forgiveness and peace.

The celebration of my fiftieth anniversary was a deep and emotive teacher. I listened. I said a thousand "thank you's." I watched people as they expressed their spirits, as their eyes welled up with tears, as they struggled to state in words the sentiments of their hearts and souls. Most of these stories revolved around a death in the family, but many were about moments of brokenness in themselves or in their marriage or in their children.

I learned in a deeper fashion the importance of the social unit called the Catholic Parish. I came to realize again that people depend on each other, on friends, on neighbors, on fellow parishioners, but they expect a kind, happy priest to be a part of the leadership and involvement in their celebrations and observances. Confidentiality is a tremendously important aspect of self-disclosure for any one of us, as we express our brokenness, our failures and our sins. This reality was demonstrated again on this past weekend several times as people thanked me for receiving their hearts and their histories in the Sacrament of Confession or in the office of the rectory.

The many expressions of kindness to me were most self-affirming and encouraging. But these expressions also taught me again of the importance of listening to the individual, especially in times of emotional stress, sadness, brokenness and failure. People repeatedly told me that I had truly listened to them. That makes me extremely happy, because somehow I had learned, over all the years of my priesthood, one of the basic needs of Gospel service, namely listening authentically to the person in my presence and in that moment.

Significant to our lives is the story line. Stories connect us as family, as friends, as associates, as loving people, as forgiving people, and as estranged people. Our stories are our history: beautiful, broken, real, and demanding of acknowledgment. Our stories as related, and as relating, experience some distortion. But generally and usually, they carry the message of the integral life that we have experienced. Our stories show us to be real and authentic.

My observance of fifty years in the priesthood of our Catholic tradition of faith has been a mirror of life. It has reflected my personal life, the life of my family, the life of the communities that I have been privileged to serve. This history teaches me and any-one who perhaps will read this journey, of the impor-tance of remembering, of reflecting, of pondering, and of describing what has been, what we have seen, how we have lived these years, and where this is leading us.

The writing of these memoirs has been, and continues to be, a prayer for me- a prayer that deepens my appreciation for my life and for the lives that have sustained, supported, forgiven, nurtured and chal-lenged me to become more than I have been. This posture and behavior have been, in my experience, a wonderful catalyst for growth and development of tal-ent, and the awareness and appreciation of persons and situations of social reality, of all of the factors in-volved in producing a healthy and happy society.

I enjoyed and appreciated every person who shared the fiftieth celebration with me, but I want to specifically mention two of the people attending the celebration. One of these people was a wonderful woman in her early nineties. She and I were speaking about how quickly life is passing for us. She said, "My grandmother used to say that days go slowly but years go quickly." We both laughed and agreed that her grandma, those many years ago, was right in her analysis of life time. This is one perception of time that I, as a priest, have dealt with through all of the years.

The other person at my reception who touched a different chord in my heart and soul regarding time was a small girl. I asked her name and she told me who she was. Then I asked how old she was. She responded, "Five-and-a-half." Then she said to me, "How old are you?" I responded that I am seventy-six years of age. She looked directly into my eyes for three or four seconds, and then said, "That's a lot!" Her parents and I enjoyed a good laugh at that moment. This child sees time and age quite differently than the elderly woman and I appreciate time!

Experiences such as these two have continued to educate me as to our humanity, as to the reality of change and growth, as to the perceptions of people about life as we all continue to age. These two people teach me again that I must listen, not only to the words in an exchange, but to the person, the circumstances, the age, and the perception involved in the exchange.

The reception held after all four parish Masses on June 4th and 5th, 2011, drew me into deep reflection about the fact that many hundreds of people with whom I have shared the past fifty years respect what I have shared with them, are very grateful for those times, and need and want to express thanks for our respective relationships.

This is one of the great rewards for me as a man and as a priest. I have been taught again that priesthood is about mystery, which is truth bigger than comprehension. Priesthood for me has been a growing experience in spirit, in mind, in relationships- and this is what I call wisdom.

Priesthood, in our Roman Catholic tradition, is about the sacred. Priesthood is about the mystery of God, about all of humanity, and about the relationships between all of God's creation and all of God's people. We celebrate and experience sacraments for every dimension of life, for all times and circumstances in life, and for all of the relationships of life. The joy of my life has largely been involved in these sacramental experiences, and these sacred experiences are largely what all the people who came to celebrate my fifty years of priesthood wanted to revisit, speak about, and remember.

My spirituality is tied closely to those people with whom I have addressed the mystery of life. Spiritual growth for me has been the focus of life. In our seminary training, we experienced disciplines that teach and demand prayer, contemplation, meditation and reflection. We also were challenged daily to manage, control, and direct our intellectual, physical, emotional, and sexual energies. We were expected to know control and direct ourselves in every dimension of life. Physical conditioning, emotional balance, and moral integrity were among the virtues upon which we were judged every day.

We also were asked to know how healthy our relationships were regarding all of our human interactions. We were expected to develop and learn stable maturity, prudent sociability, balanced psychology and a rich and sustaining spirituality. Eight years of seminary training emphasized these areas of growth and development in order that we could be healthy, happy, and ready to share with people in all of the joy, sorrow, trauma and experience of the human journey.

I remember a wonderful spiritual director, Msgr. John Gregoir, who was my director from 1953 through 1957, during the first four years of seminary training. He spoke often about the fact that we, as priests, would be called upon to participate in and deal with every conceivable human condition, experience, emotion, reaction. In our psychology and spiritual training we were reminded frequently that we would deal daily with human failure, betrayal and weakness, our own and these conditions in others. We were challenged to develop a healthy and stable spirituality, awareness and alertness, in order to effectively direct our own lives and the lives of those people we served.

Priests also deal with the beauty, strength, wisdom and integrity of people, but more often than not, the priest is called when some person, some relationship, some family is seriously broken or wounded. Maturity, spiritual integrity and emotional stability are the tools that I have had to work at for fifty years. I pray God that, for the most part, I have behaved in a human, compassionate, and priestly fashion.

As a general rule we avoid exposing our failures, our weaknesses, or sins, or our pain to others. In our Catholic tradition over the centuries, a trust has been built up, as I see it, in the Sacrament of Confession, or as this experience is currently known, the Sacrament of Reconciliation. People do trust this sacred experience, and bring their most secret and painful dimensions to the priest in this setting. Earlier in these memoirs, I mentioned that Msgr. McGinnis, my Latin professor in college, once told my classmates and me that the most important tool for a priest to perfect to help people is the willingness and ability to listen. Fifty years of experience have taught me that he was totally correct in his assessment.

CHAPTER 32

Weekday Mass

I offered weekday Mass this morning (6/14/11) at St. Pius X Church with about sixty people, mostly the same people who are present at Mass every weekday at St. Pius X Church. These wonderful people are young and old, professional and blue-collar, and of many other categorical descriptions. They come to pray, to reflect, to experience silence, and to support each other. They presumably come for comfort, for growth, for nurturance, and to experience a faith-filled community, among other possibilities. They come to celebrate the Sacrament of Reconciliation, which we offer every day for one-half hour before the 8:00 Mass. Many people enter into this prayerful experience of alleviating guilt, of admitting failure, and of renewing their souls for the life ahead. This sacramental experience for me, as a confessor, is profoundly rich, humbling, and challenging to listen attentively to the heart being offered and expressed in humble prayer, the prayer of confessing failure and sin.

No one is challenged to be present for this daily prayerful experience. This is why their presence gives me, as celebrant of the Mass, a deep gift of spirituality, support, and encouragement. I am easily distracted by the pain that I deal with in individual people's lives, as confessor and as counselor, and in the social pain that is described graphically every day on television and radio. Faith practice gives me a stability, a solid foundation, a willingness to continue to enter the pain of lives, the sadness of lives, the contradictions and failures of lives, and the sin and selfishness of life. This experience includes my own weaknesses, failures, sins and limitations, as it involves those of the people who approach me as pastor, as confessor, and as counselor.

After fifty and more years as a priest, I am learning more completely that the Gospel truth, which has been a life-long companion, and the Eucharistic experience, which also has been a life-long comforting practice, are the lifeblood of my spirit as a human being, as a Christian, and as a priest. These basic spiritual rituals and practices are profoundly powerful in restoring me to balance, to deepening, to enrichment, and to renewal of my soul for the practice of life, of goodness, of kindness, and of forgiveness.

These are among the basic teachings of Jesus. These are the life-giving and life-preserving practices which we espouse and try to teach, and more importantly, try to live every day, as we practice our Christian faith.

Stages of Life

As I experienced my celebrations of fifty years as a priest on June 4th and 5th, 2011, I became more aware than ever of how young people are inspired to persevere in their efforts to remain faithful to the journey which they choose. Many young people told me that my life is a challenge to them to remain faithful to their beliefs and to persevere in overcoming the difficulties that are part of every human life. I am learning that older life speaks in perseverance, in example, and in inspiration, more than in the lectures we give, in the homilies we preach, or in the advice we offer. I am learning again, and more completely, that being speaks louder than words.

I have learned at the fiftieth celebration of my priesthood that younger people are inspired, that they stand in awe, that they ponder what fifty years of anything is about. The teachings of life happen in the younger people experiencing the older people more than in the younger people listening to the older people. Again, actions speak louder than words. I know that verbal exchange between people is extremely important, but example speaks louder than any verbal advice. Jesus taught that we should teach by being, by acting, and by believing.

As I grow older as a human being and as a priest, I am learning that history matters- human history, family history, and personal history. Our life journey and track record teach and inspire, or shame and condemn, humanity and the aspirations and hopes of humanity. We, by our life stories, either add to or detract from the human situation and condition of our brothers and sisters around the world.

Aging has assisted me in accepting the limitations of my body, mind and spirit. I am still blessed with strength in all of these categories, but I am learning continuously and continually that changes are happening at what appears to be an accelerating pace. We learn the path of life by walking it. Never has this been more true for me than in the last few years.

I learn all along the way that I must open myself to new definitions of life, new dimensions of life, new limits in life, and new radical changes in life. I am no longer as physically strong, as mentally capable, as emotionally pliable, or as spiritually dynamic as I was a few years ago. But I am also learning that my current condition is the place where I meet God, where I experience life, where my spirit grows, and where I touch and teach people. I am experiencing the fact that my life continues to contribute to the social fabric, to individual persons, and to my own spirit, as I learn to live differently.

Each new dimension and experience of my life has been a point in time for reflection. For the first part of my life, I was accelerating, accomplishing, and succeeding in all of my assignments and responsibilities. I was alert, capable, and energetic. I attacked each new assignment with vigor, with prudence, and with determination. My bishops somehow knew that I could and would tackle any problem. They knew that I would move into difficult situations with determination. I did that a few times in my priestly career. I would not change that history. It made me who I am today.

As a priest, my life unfolded as the bishop directed. I had promised obedience on the day that I was ordained, and I took that promise seriously. I was assigned to many different responsibilities. I enjoyed every single one of them, and I learned from them.

As I conclude these memoirs to date, June 16, 2011, I am grateful for a life that was full of experiences, opportunities, challenges, and unbelievable rewards, as I lived out my priesthood. I have experienced humility in my weaknesses, and this has em-

powered me to help others in their failures. I have
known discouragement when life did not flow as I
wanted when I was involved and making every effort
to direct life as I saw it for self and for others. I have
learned perseverance through the difficult social problems and issues with which I was involved all through
the years. I have learned patience by the flow of life in
Church functions and living, just exactly as life is in
us human beings, beautiful, present, and flawed by
poor choices, by imprudent decisions and flawed
thinking.

I have also learned gratitude for the beauty of
the lives of people with whom I have worked over all
the years. I have learned the dignity of human life,
and of all of life, as the years have unfolded and presented me with visions, opportunities and challenges
to engage life in a productive way, so as to increase
this rich gift of God among us at every moment of our
existence.

Life as a priest has deepened my appreciation
of our human nature, beautiful and made in God's image; and sinful, in need of constant management, discipline, and direction as we together work out our salvation. I have come to appreciate more than ever in
my life the concept of "The Body of Christ." We are
all one, one with God, one with each other, and one
with all of creation. We are one in the Lord, and our

call is to continually work at that unity. I appreciate that I have experienced the life of being at the center of the Gospel, at the core of the Eucharist, involved in all of the sacraments. What a privilege it is to share with others these sacred moments and experiences.

As I wind down my life, I am thankful, I am excited, I am curious for the next chapter. Diminishing physical strength, diminishing mental acuity and awareness, and diminishing energy in all of the areas of previous experience are definitive calls to reexamine where I am, where I am going, how I see all of this movement, and what this means for the present moment. I am learning the path of aging as I walk it. This journey is threatening, inspiring, mysterious, exciting, and inevitable. Each of us must deal with the movement toward the end of life on this planet, and as we have known life to be. This is the new launching pad for life into the future, into eternity, into the mystery of God's plan for each of us and for all of creation. This journey teaches us totally that we are participants in the mysterious journey of existence. We do not direct the energy, we do not determine the outcome, we do not know what is at stake, but we participate in this wonderful and mysterious experience of continuance into the next chapter of our existence.

How thankful I am to my parents, to my brothers, to my teachers, to my friends, and to all the people with whom I have shared life, if only for a second, in holding a door open, in smiling in a passing moment, in exchanging a look, a word, a moment, as we live out this existence. I am more aware now than ever before that I am one with the universe, one with the reality of living and dying, and one with the eternal existence that has been, is, and will be, continuously and mysteriously.

Mortality

As experiences come into life for me, I appreciate more than ever before that life is a treasure as I understand it and as I experience it. Life is profoundly mysterious in its human experiential beginnings, in its destiny, in its offerings all along the way of temporal engagement. Eternity, as we Christians speak of it, is a part of the mystery.

Each of us will die. Each of us, throughout life, has many emotional, psychological, and spiritual experiences, thoughts, and emotions about this reality. We are not in charge of this reality. We do not understand it. We fear what is not in our control. We ponder what we and others should expect and prepare for regarding death.

I am convinced that how we deal with our mortality defines to a great degree how we live life, how we appreciate our time here on earth, and how we develop a spiritual life plan for our journey. We live with the reality of mortality from the time that we come to the age of reason. The awareness, willingness to dialogue about this phenomenon, and openness to all the possibilities held in the experience of dying, are aspects of the energy that forms our everyday experience of life. In other words, I believe that how we perceive life and how we address death are very important dimensions of the definition of our life experience. Our spiritual, emotional, intuitional and social involvements and awareness are extremely important for our happiness all along the way.

This reality, in my estimation, is why frequent, weekly worship is so important. Our condition as humans seems to call for the fact that we need spiritual nurturance frequently, just as we need bodily nurturance and care continuously, in order to live as healthy, potentially happy human beings. We learn, as we grow, that we have a body and that we are a spirit. Both dimensions, body and spirit, need continued attention if we hope to expect growth, fulfillment and peace of mind.

Experience, development, maturation and change are very important reflective platforms for our growth. As we age, and as we experience each new phase of life, we are changed in our emotional, spiritual, intellectual and social approach to the life we have been given, in this time and as of these circumstances. It strikes me that humility is a very important piece of the equation that brings us to the involvement and experience of addressing the mystery of existence, of existence itself, and of our part in this existence. We are humble participants in life; we are not prime movers of life.

These thoughts, feelings, and intuitions are my companions as I grow older. I am much at peace with this setting. My life has been rich and continues to be fulfilling. This is a great blessing.

FINIS